SICKNESS IN STYLE

Nica Cornell

SICKNESS IN STYLE

A Memoir of Distress and Dislocation through Dress

Fashion and Personal Style Studies
Collection Editor

Joseph H. Hancock II

First published in 2025 by Lived Places Publishing

All rights reserved. No part of this publication may be reproduced, stored in a retrieval system, or transmitted in any form or by any means, electronic, mechanical, photocopying, recording, or otherwise, without prior permission in writing from the publisher.

No part of this book may be used or reproduced in any manner for the purpose of training artificial intelligence technologies or systems. In accordance with Article 4(3) of the Digital Single Market Directive 2019/790, Lived Places Publishing expressly reserves this work from the text and data mining exception.

The author and editor have made every effort to ensure the accuracy of the information contained in this publication but assume no responsibility for any errors, inaccuracies, inconsistencies, or omissions. Likewise, every effort has been made to contact copyright holders. If any copyright material has been reproduced unwittingly and without permission, the publisher will gladly receive information enabling them to rectify any error or omission in subsequent editions.

Copyright © 2025 Lived Places Publishing

British Library Cataloguing in Publication Data
A CIP record for this book is available from the British Library.

ISBN: 9781916985186 (pbk)
ISBN: 9781916985209 (ePDF)
ISBN: 9781916985193 (ePUB)

The right of Nica Cornell to be identified as the Author of this work has been asserted by them in accordance with the Copyright, Design and Patents Act 1988.

Cover design by Fiachra McCarthy
Book design by Rachel Trolove of Twin Trail Design
Typeset by Newgen Publishing, UK

Lived Places Publishing
P.O. Box 1845
47 Echo Avenue
Miller Place, NY 11764

www.livedplacespublishing.com

To David, *vir alles*

Abstract

Navigating the development of her disabling mental illness from her home in South Africa to university in Oxford and recovery in London, author Nica Cornell uses the garments she travelled with to reflect on her experience. Cornell explores the effect of garments such as her Ankara sheath dress, sub fusc, and second-hand clothing, and how they influenced her experience of alienation, exclusion, and realisation.

Sickness in Style explores the challenges of dressing and how it can become an obstacle to accessing the external world, as well as how beauty can be rediscovered through second-hand outfits. This book is ideal reading for students of Fashion Studies, Disability Studies, Psychology, and Migration Studies.

Key words

Fashion, lived experience, disability, recovery, PTSD, panic attacks, relationships, immigration, accessibility, second-hand fashion, dress

Contents

Content warning	x
Introduction	xi
Learning objectives	xiv
Part I	1
Chapter 1 International student orientation: Oxford, England	3
Chapter 2 Sub fusc: Oxford, England	9
Chapter 3 Dinner with the Provost: Oxford, England	11
Chapter 4 Legally disabled: Oxford, England	19
Chapter 5 Going home: Alice, South Africa	25
Chapter 6 Taxing travel: Ealing, London	33
Chapter 7 Moving in: Ealing, London	37
Chapter 8 A porcelain pillbox: Ealing, London	43
Chapter 9 Exotic Ealing: Ealing, London	47
Chapter 10 Five roses: Ealing, London	51
Chapter 11 Walking in Walpole: Ealing, London	55
Chapter 12 Alone and unsafe: Ealing, London	57
Chapter 13 Mary's Living & Giving: Ealing, London	61
Chapter 14 Calleycat the alleycat: Ealing, London	63
Chapter 15 Medication: Ealing, London	67

Chapter 16	Medical illness: Ealing, London	**71**
Chapter 17	Don't lock the door: Ealing, London	**75**
Part II		**77**
Chapter 18	Elegance in Ealing: Ealing, London	**79**
Chapter 19	Foreign fiancée: Ealing, London	**85**
Chapter 20	Engaged: Ealing, London	**87**
Chapter 21	Stuttering shame: Ealing, London	**89**
Chapter 22	Paperwork purgatory: Ealing, London	**91**
Chapter 23	Elegance in Ealing continued: Ealing, London	**95**
Chapter 24	Breaking up on the bus: Bristol, London	**101**
Chapter 25	Elegance in Ealing continued: Ealing, London	**105**
Chapter 26	Pregnancy scare: Ealing, London	**109**
Chapter 27	Trousseau: Ealing, London	**115**
Chapter 28	Morning of marriage: Ealing, London	**121**
Chapter 29	Civil ceremony: Haringey, London	**127**
Chapter 30	Reception: Richmond, London	**131**
Chapter 31	Wife: Ealing, London	**135**
Chapter 32	Immigrant: Croydon, London	**137**
Chapter 33	New job: Ealing, London	**141**
Chapter 34	Newlywed: Ealing, London	**143**
Chapter 35	Elegance in Ealing continued: Ealing, London	**145**
Chapter 36	Calamity: Ealing, London	**147**

Chapter 37	Pandemic: Ealing, London	**149**
Chapter 38	Elegance in Ealing continued: Ealing, London	**153**
Chapter 39	A visa: Ealing, London	**155**
Chapter 40	Conclusion: London, England	**159**
Notes		**163**
Suggested discussion topics		**164**
References		**165**
Index		**167**

Content warning

This book contains explicit references to, and descriptions of, situations which may cause distress. This includes references to and descriptions of:

- Suicidal thoughts and intentions
- Complex post-traumatic stress disorder
- Ableism, discrimination, and microaggressions
- Medical negligence
- Immigration trauma

Please be aware that references to potentially distressing topics occur **frequently** and **throughout** the book.

Introduction

A floor length sequined white evening gown, worn with a silk, hot pink shirt & feather boa.

A rented evening gown from Sue Farmer – the costume hire place down the road in Pinelands, a suburb of Cape Town, South Africa. One of my favourite places in the world. I wanted to be Sue – to have access to that array of selves. For we are transformed by dress. I remember the titillation of picking out the outfit, as much as I remember the party – and not only because I had far too much tequila. I couldn't help it. The others couldn't be left to do shots alone, and I'd made two house rules for my farewell party at the colourful house on Riverside Drive.

1. Be nice to my cats

2. Take a shot if you mention Oxford.

I hadn't even been there yet, but I was already *gatvol* (the Afrikaans word for fed up which translates directly as 'full of holes') of the glassy-eyed look people got when they spoke about it. It was just another university to me.

You'd think I'd have learned my lesson from four years at Rhodes University in Grahamstown, now Makhanda. How we fought for a name change, among many other things. To no longer be educated in the name of a white supremacist who epitomised colonialism and imperialism. Because symbols matter – especially when they are on fucking everything. The Black Student Movement, of which I was a member, saw many vital victories and many painful losses. I was hospitalised with major depressive disorder and intermittent anxiety within six months of completing my Honours degree in Political and International Studies at Rhodes. Maybe it's like labour, some surge of hormones makes you forget the pain? So, it's an achievement to be alive two years later, in my sparkly dress at my Mamma Mia themed farewell party, about to leave for a master's in another country. It seems too simple to claim ignorance now. But I wanted to study again and was too traumatised to return to the South African university landscape at that point. My boyfriend lived in London, and I wanted to give us a shot. I needed distance from my parents. I didn't understand the collegiate system – I didn't even know the word.

Now, I wonder how I could not have done more research. Perhaps because I knew that if I did, I wouldn't have the courage to get on the plane. I already had my doubts. I wanted to go to SOAS, or Goldsmiths, where I'd gotten in but not received funding. It was the notoriously conservative Oxford that offered a scholarship. I hoped that by studying African Studies, I'd be surrounded by students with common interests, at least. I'd remain connected to my continent – because place matters too. We live in our bodies, then in that with which we adorn them, then in a place.

I was raised by anti-apartheid activist parents. I understood I was South African before I was anything else. I had a responsibility to my country – more so, because I am white. People who looked like me had plundered and damaged this place that birthed me. I had a responsibility to try, in some small way, to be better than the history I carried in my body. For better or for worse. And things were about to get worse.

Learning objectives

- How can immigration impact physical and mental health?
- How does disability affect one's relationship with dress?
- How can dress be a source of comfort and resilience when grappling with trauma?

Part I

1
International student orientation: Oxford, England

An off the shoulder black cotton top I'd owned for a decade. Cerulean blue jeans. A sling bag in a red, yellow & black Ankara fabric.

I dress for the orientation day for international students at the University of Oxford – in the dark of early autumn, in an Airbnb that is a kind lady's second bedroom in the next town over. My scholarship money hasn't come in yet, and we can't afford the accommodation in the town itself. It has taken everything I've earned just to get here, what with application, travel and visa fees (which included a lung scan to prove I don't have tuberculosis and an English test – my two degrees from an

English-medium university, and a decade long publication record were insufficient).

I notice a hole in the elastic of my white cotton panties, and this ordinary detail looms large in my mind – such a stark contrast to the grandeur and scale of the buildings I spied from the bus the afternoon before. I feel extraordinarily small in comparison, and that is before I arrive at the Examination Schools building on High Street and see the plaque to Cecil John Rhodes on the wall. I already know about the statue they'd refused to take down when the Rhodes Must Fall movement reached Oxford. But nobody has mentioned the plaque.

I have already written my poem *CJR*[1], to process the traumas I experienced during my time in the Rhodes Must Fall movement.

> *They say Cecil John Rhodes didn't like women.*
> *He dogs me.*
> *I've known his name longer than I've known it was*
>   *one.*
> *Before they put the wires in, whenever I close my*
>   *mouth (often)*
> *my bottom teeth dig small troughs in His gums*
> *my father drives me*
>   *on His avenue*
>   *to the house*
>   *where he left me behind*
>   *(he remembers the plants/not his seed.)*
> *When I am listening to my history teacher*
>   *tell me I deserve to be someone's mother/*
>   *someone's wife, thinking I should write this*
>   *down before I forget I'm worthy*

> *He is ripping my skirt to show my thighs aren't*
> *as smooth as my prose.*
> *After I fled to the closest border town,*
> *tried to love a man who needs a mother and a*
> *wife (but not me)*
> *tried to love a cause who needs a writer and a*
> *student (but not me)*
> *He claps as the Vice Chancellor calls my*
> *name/the dogs.*

That line… "I've known his name longer than I've known it was one," is not poetic licence. I grew up off Rhodes Avenue in University Estate, Cape Town. We walked in the forest and climbed on the lion statues at Rhodes Memorial. At high school, we were taught about him as some kind of hero and I remember writing an essay and being vaguely impressed. My mom, on the other hand, was decidedly not impressed with what we were being taught. We visited the cottage where he died the peaceful death he denied others. My aunt is an oral historian, who has interviewed people who are employed as domestic workers, farm labourers, gardeners, nuns, and priests. She argues with the people at Rhodes Cottage, which is just around the corner from where she lives, disputing the narrative they are peddling. Studying a year of art history in my undergraduate degree at Rhodes University, I was set the task of how we would transform the space of what in Cape Town was affectionately known as 'Rhodes Mem'.

I am of the post-colony. Our symbolic landscape is contradictory. There's such a preoccupation with the notion that taking down statues is 'erasing history'. I wish that history could be erased. But whether we prop up these towers of stone, or tear them down, that history is alive in the everyday life of South Africans and Zimbabweans.

I last half a day in Oxford that first day, then cannot take it anymore and flee back to my boyfriend's student flat in Ealing, London.

2
Sub fusc: Oxford, England

I learn the term 'sub fusc,' short for sub fuscus meaning dark brown in Latin. This mandatory outfit entails black skirt or trousers; plain white collared shirts with sleeves; black academic gown and mortar board; black ribbon tie, and black stockings or socks.

*'Socks, tights and stockings **must** be worn and must cover the ankle entirely. There should be no gap between the bottom of the trouser leg or skirt and the top of the socks or stockings' (University of Oxford, 2022).*

Whole adults are sent to change their socks on the day.

New students stand in spindling queues in the rain, waiting to be admitted, to wind up a scruffy narrow wooden staircase and cram in beneath the grand, ornately decorated dome of the Sheldonian Theatre. The brief minutes of the ensuing matriculation ceremony feel like being initiated into a cult. I am utterly saturated by the scale of the space and its overwhelming grandeur; the ancient language of Latin hanging in the air as alchemy and the mass constituted by the audience's uniform dress. I am reminded of nothing so much as attending Mass as a child with my Catholic granny, and not understanding the priest. But this is an institution of education, of critical thinking, or so it has proclaimed. Not this mass performance of uniformity and alienation. By the time the Vice-Chancellor speaks in English to say that we are all now members of Oxford for life, I am already wondering if I want to be.

3
Dinner with the Provost: Oxford, England

A maroon sheath dress in Ankara fabric, with a pattern of mielies, or corncobs. I had it made in Kinshasa, Democratic Republic of Congo (DRC), when I visited with my Congolese-South African best friend after finishing my Honours degree. This was the dress I had worn beneath my academic gown to my postgraduate graduation ceremony in South Africa.

My College, I quickly discover, is notoriously conservative – even for Oxford. As part of my pre-arrival pack, they send me a notice saying there are embroidery classes available if I am bringing a partner from South Africa. The implied assumption that the student would be a man was not so far out of line with what I was told when I got there – that 1985 was when my College first let women in. Well, my boyfriend lives in London, is a six-foot man, and probably would enjoy an embroidery class or two. The pack also told me that there would be various formal occasions. I packed all my most formal clothing, most of which are cocktail dresses I'd had made in Ghana and the DRC in Ankara fabric. That and a ballgown I'd worn to my matriculation dance, among other events – a raw silk gown with a boned bodice and sweetheart neckline, and a tiered skirt with layers of patterned organza. For us, matriculation was the end of high school.

There are no other African Studies students in my College, and only one or two of colour – including a Ugandan student who tells me I am the first person he'd met who knew what (not where, what) Uganda was.

I make a friend from Luxembourg studying Migration Studies while queuing for the most patronising presentation on mental health I can imagine. I've lived with major depressive disorder, and anxiety, since I was a child – I am only two years out of the hospital where they found the medication that saved my life.

Thankfully I am not living on the main site of the College, where I stray onto the grass once and am shouted at by a man actually wearing a three-piece tweed suit that, "We do not walk on the grass." Somehow the weight of being a walking caricature has yet to wear him down. I am living, along with many postgraduates, at James Mellon Hall on Rectory Road in Cowley. This part of town feels more normal to me, and I breathe easier when I get over the bridge into it. I meet people who look at me askance when I tell them I live in Cowley.

I am invited to my first College dinner, wearing my academic gown over formal dress. I purposefully wear my maroon Ankara dress printed with *mielies* (Afrikaans for corncobs), to assert – mostly for myself – that it is possible to bring my politics and identity into the strained halls of Oriel. It is already becoming apparent that this is not the case. On coming into the formally dressed hall, which I notice has a stained-glass window dedicated to Rhodes, I am directed to the head table that sits at a perpendicular angle to the long tables of students and staff. I thought I'd be sitting with my new friend from Luxembourg. But I seem to have been allocated a seat right next to the Provost, who – no kidding – has a gavel in reach. I sit down at the table, and he asks me where I am from. I say South Africa. His response with a wag of his finger is, "None of that Rhodes nonsense from you." Any hope I had left that this place would be different, that maybe I could be myself here, is swiftly pulverised.

It is an excruciating dinner, lukewarm pigeon and popcorn sauce aside. I try to explain, while acutely conscious that my visa depends on my scholarship which comes from the College, why this is not ancient history for us. The weight of it. To say enough that I don't feel a total traitor for sitting here at all. He quite clearly finds it entertaining.

After, I strip the dress off in my new friend's room on the main site like it is on fire. I won't wear it again. Its vibrant colours vibrate before my mind's eye when I picture that night, the brilliant gold corncob dissolving into the shadows of all that is unspoken in that hall.

I walk home, chest heaving with tears, and the next day flee once again to Ealing.

That weekend, while my boyfriend is at work, I take myself to the local Iranian restaurant on New Broadway, Boof. The tension is still in my body. I pour it out onto the page, beginning what would become a letter I know I have to send for my sense of self-worth.

> *Dear Sir*
> *We were seated beside each other at the Postgraduate Freshers Dinner which, to the amusement of the Hall, you joked "must have been some kind of test." I presume you meant for you, yet it has proved my most difficult test since arriving at Oxford.*
> *We had two conversations, one about Rhodes Must Fall and one about mental health, which for me and many of my friends are indelibly linked. You were impressed, and seemingly moved, by my progress since being hospitalised in 2016.*
> *But as Provost of a college, even one as notoriously conservative as Oriel, which holds in your words from that night, publicly pointing to my student activism as an example, 'a diverse range of students,' you have a responsibility to understand the potential implications of the power dynamic in the place.*
> *I tried my best to answer your questions honestly and with integrity, and I listened as you told me how hard the College*

had found being forced to grapple with Rhodes' legacy of white supremacy. I have located and read the statement on Oriel's website as you recommended. As a South African, I find it sorely lacking – most prominently, in how it casts this debate as abstract and of the past, as opposed to a legacy that, as I said to you, evokes such strong feeling because it is still affects people's everyday experiences and lives.

But we do not need to agree on this. I simply need you to hear that in the Hall, in a building that he funded that blithely celebrated him until it was challenged not to, when you turn to a new African student, who is on a scholarship, and say, 'None of that Rhodes nonsense from you,' it is an exercise in power. And a reminder to me that the last time I went to a university, in my case named after him, it called policemen with dogs on its students. You do not have to intend malice to do harm.

The best way I have to demonstrate this to you is to explain what the days since have been like. I sobbed while walking home that night, and every night since. I had such a severe anxiety attack the next day that I had to withdraw from my obligations at the African Studies Centre. The same thing happened in class yesterday, to the extent that I found myself on my knees in my classroom scrambling for a tranquiliser. It is taking every trick in my book to resist a depressive episode, my first in two years. There has been no time for the actual academic work I came here for as I have been totally consumed by the emotional labour of deciding whether I can bear to stay.

I am well aware that this will probably be startling to you as I sat and politely engaged in conversation. But my response to trauma being triggered is to endure it, until I can get somewhere where it is safe to feel it. And in that room, in this College, in this town, it has felt as if there is nowhere that is safe.

I do not hold you responsible for the traumas of my past. But I expect you, as my Provost, to take the power and privilege of your position seriously and consider the scale and scope of its implications.

4
Legally disabled: Oxford, England

Cheap silver rings I previously wore as symbols of protection in my first job after the hospital, as a salesperson in Bargain Books in Pinelands. In Oxford, I find they've lost whatever juice they once had.

Oxford is a blur of illness, set to the two songs I play over and over again, *Take Me Home* by Jess Glynne and *Read All About It* by Emeli Sandé.

My body disappears as another swims into view. This new body has multiple, unpredictable panic attacks and hot flushes each day. Its arms strip off loose layers in order to breathe. Its hands tremble. It has to be rescued by strangers from the middle of the road when its knees shake and its legs cannot move. It has to wear running shoes because its balance is tenuous. It cannot go to shops alone. Noise of any kind is unbearable, rendering it frantic. It stutters or cannot speak at all. It stretches as movement becomes harder and cooking requires standing for too long. It goes swimming, in a hand-me-down navy one-piece that is becoming too tight, to try to regulate breathing. One day it simply sinks in the pool.

Legally, in the United Kingdom, my longstanding mental illness designates me as disabled. I accepted that language for the first time on all the forms I filled in before travelling, seeking to ensure that proper support would be put in place. By the beginning of the second term, I am as exhausted by the extra labour of trying to access support as I am by my condition. Despite my efforts, I continue to feel, for the most part, unheard and unsupported. Eventually, after it turns out my carefully crafted Student Support Plan simply never even reached the right people in my department, I find myself pouring it out on the page again:

> *Thank you for getting back to me. I am glad to hear it has been taken seriously and measures have been taken so this will not happen again.*

That being said, I remain incredibly frustrated with the way my mental health has been mismanaged by the University. As my psychologist pointed out, such mistakes when you are dealing with someone with a history of clinical depression quite literally puts their life at risk.

I was extremely careful in my decision to attend university in a foreign country. It took a year and a half after my Honours degree to ensure that my health was stable enough to contemplate such a decision, and another year of preparation and extraordinary effort to arrive here, able and well enough to do my master's. I disclosed my condition from the beginning. As someone who has experienced the stigma associated with mental health, this is no easy task. I was immensely relieved when we spoke on the phone while I was still in South Africa, and the Student Support Plan system was explained to me and put in place. It was a deciding factor.

Yet my health has been compromised from the word go. While many people are well-intentioned, there seems to be little thorough understanding of what it is to have students with such conditions studying here.

The very steps that you mention entail more administration and emotional labour on my part. This has been my experience at every stage of the various processes that I seem to be constantly engaged in to get the support I need. Despite my condition being on record, and my putting considerable effort into keeping the various people involved up to date with what is happening (a process that in itself is deeply retraumatising), I am asked again and again to fill out forms describing my condition and how it affects my work and life. The list of strangers I have had to share this with is by now absurdly long. I am Cc-ing in this mail the whittled down list of people that it has finally come to – after weeks of me seeking help at every turn last term. It still includes my disability mentor, you as my disability advisor, and the disability co-ordinator at my College, and my departmental supervisor. This is outside of my having to be in contact with the GP here, as well as my psychiatrist and psychologist at home, and all of the secondary layers of communication I have to engage in to try and get problems solved – the IT guys who were once again in my room on Wednesday and still have not managed to fix the internet so that I can Skype with my psychologist, the Treasury Assistant managing hardship funding applications, each lecturer I had last term, the Lodge employee who insisted that 'health' is not sufficient reason to require a taxi, and the list goes on.

This is not just a question of the SSP not being managed correctly. The process of submitting a mitigating circumstances form, or a hardship funding application to cover psychotherapy, or accessing the taxi service that was set up, is as filled with anxiety as anything else – when each day I am already constantly making calculations based on whether or not I might have an attack.

My condition was considered in remission before I arrived here. I am of course aware that the stress of the transition would have come with some natural challenges, and that I had a particularly difficult start with a traumatising incident with the Provost of my College – in stark contrast to the welfare talk given at the College the very night before. But the ongoing mismanagement and misunderstanding puts me in a situation where there are significantly more days with anxiety attacks than without, and each day I have to consider how likely it is that I will once again have to deal with the humiliation of getting on my knees in the elevator in front of my classmates because I can't stand I'm shaking so much.

As such, I am exhausted. At this stage, I do not want to speak to more strangers about my most private experiences, I do not want to fill in more forms, I do not want to disclose the name of the lecturer I had to educate about how mental illness is not something you just "overcome".

All I want is to do my work, and all I have asked for is help in being able to do that when my disease makes things harder through no fault of my own. Instead of making it easier, it has repeatedly been made harder.

I understand that these various systematic failures are no one person's fault. But I am tired of being understanding; or having to say thank you for help I was promised; or thinking good intentions are good enough. They are not.

This university put my life at risk last term. I told over 10 members of staff what was happening, and it took the entire term to find one, my departmental supervisor, who actually took my condition sufficiently seriously.

Oxford is either equipped to support students with disabilities, or it is not.

If it is not then it is negligent and dangerous to pretend it is.
Nica Cornell

5
Going home: Alice, South Africa

Three quarter fitted black cotton leggings that get me unwelcome attention in the small, remote town where I'm doing research.

I travel home for fieldwork – flying with a new South African friend from university. I'm only going to be allowed to fly, because she is also going home for fieldwork and we coordinate so we're on the same plane. My departmental supervisor is so concerned about my health by this point that she does not consider it safe for me to fly alone. She is right but this is part of the unravelling of my life – I flew into London alone six months ago. I flew into Accra alone at 18, to be a human rights volunteer.

I flew into Paris alone at 16, to fulfil my dream of seeing Notre Dame, paying for my own dream trip to Paris with my earnings from my writing. Each detail was terrifying in its magnitude – I vividly remember not knowing how to use the taps in the aeroplane bathroom, and having to ask an air hostess how while oozing with embarrassment; having to clamber over the giant sleeping man in the seat next to me to go to the bathroom, after he had told me he was a bodyguard for an autocratic monarchy; being so paralysed in Dubai airport by the awareness that there was no-one I knew on the entire continent, that I sat and read an entire *Mills & Boon* at my gate six hours early; and finally, ravenous, that I navigated the extraordinarily long route between my gate and the food court six times without summoning the courage to actually buy anything. It was terrifying, no doubt. But it was also exhilarating. Because I did it without worrying about falling down, or having to type out a heart-crumbling message on my phone for the flight attendant that I was having an attack and couldn't speak. A decade later, eight years into adulthood, the independent streak that sent me to Accra, Ghana, for three months at 18, and made me go to a university on the other side of the country, has been worn away.

I told someone about catching the bus to the Ghanaian border, crossing into Lomé, Togo's capital, on foot. I told him about being fleeced of a third of our money as we got off the bus by the currency traders; being asked for a bribe by the Ghanaian official who also casually asked me to marry him while holding my passport in his hand; about managing with my friend Alex's partial French; and how the city had an urgency to it that was a little bit frightening. (Note: this is not a summary of my experience there. These are the tough bits, relevant to the broader point. This shouldn't need specifying, but people assume stupid shit about African countries.)

"Two white girls…and you thought you'd go to Togo for the weekend, on your own? Why?" It wasn't an original question – the police officers who pulled us out of the *tro-tro* on our way back and wouldn't let us retrieve our stuff (including our passports, money and volunteer IDs) seemed to have much the same thing on their mind.

Because we wanted to. We could. I could.

Now, eight years into adulthood, it is considered unsafe for me to fly alone.

Before I fly, my boyfriend David writes a letter to my closest family and friends in South Africa so they know what to expect. He knows more than I do about my own body's symptoms at this point.

> Nica's anxiety disorder has recently developed, into what her psychiatrists have diagnosed as a panic disorder. This means that her symptoms and triggers have changed somewhat, and may be different than you are used to. I'm writing this letter because I have been the closest to her as she has gone through this process. This way she does not have to revisit the experience or explain multiple times when she arrives in South Africa. All she has to do is focus on her work and enjoy her loved ones.
>
> Perhaps largest among her new symptoms are the physical aspects. She may at times experience profuse sweating, or shaking. However, this does not necessarily mean she is feeling panic. Sometimes she is just as surprised as anyone else. You don't need to take action unless you sense that she has been quiet for a while, or her eyes have been fixed on one point for an unusually long period of time.
>
> It is also important always to ask whether she is feeling panic first, in a non-obtrusive way. Just a simple "are you feeling okay?" or "do you want to go somewhere quiet?" If she does not say she is having an attack, don't push her. Just stay nearby and make sure she knows you are there to support her. After a while you can ask again, still

unobtrusively. She may say that she needs help, but if she still doesn't, don't push. Eventually, she will tell you what she needs, or manage to regain her calm.

Once she does tell you she is having an attack, there are a couple of things you can do. First and foremost is to isolate her to a place she feels safe. When Nica is having an attack she feels like she is about to be violated and attacked. She feels completely unsafe, so helping her regain control is paramount. If she can retreat to a quiet, familiar place, she can normally do this herself over time. If there isn't a familiar place available, if you are out in public for example, try to find a nice, quiet, decently empty spot. Also, if it is feasible, suggest going home, but do not push that option. Just let her know it is available.

If you have tranquilisers with you, you can offer her one. Never force it on her though, the option must always be hers. Nica doesn't enjoy taking lots of pills (who does?) so this is generally a last resort, especially in public. Always try to make her feel safe first, and then if the attack is going long (generally over half an hour), suggest a tranquiliser. If she says no, then the answer is no. She may have other ideas about how to manage her anxiety. Do not ask again unless you are at home, in a safe space, and the attack is still really bad after a while.

Sometimes when she is having an attack, she does not like to be touched. If she seems obviously skittish while doing her breathing, it might not be a good idea to add more physical stimuli. There's nothing wrong with asking if you're not sure, just a simple "Is it okay if I touch you?" before holding her hand, or putting your arm around her for physical comfort. Again though, do not push. If she doesn't answer, it means that the answer is no or she is not yet at a place to formulate sentences. Asking repeatedly will only make matters worse. Give her space.

As you may know, she is on a new medication that helps alleviate physical triggers, but some of these may still occur from time to time. Noise is a big one. If you are on a very noisy street, with a lot of sudden bangs and shouts, there's a chance it could trigger an attack. Additionally, large crowds, or huge stores. While it's important to be aware of these things, it is equally important not to let them have dominion over the activities that you and Nica do together. Nothing frustrates and angers Nica more than her condition getting in the way of her life. Always empower her to make her own calls on what she can and cannot do. If you guys are planning to go to a Mall, literally the worst thing you can say is "No you can't because large crowds give you attacks." Also, these triggers have been somewhat alleviated because of the recent change in medication.

When Nica is having an attack, she is not able to tell you what she needs. That can sometimes seem a bit scary or confusing, but the point is that her brain literally feels like it is screaming at her. She can't formulate ideas very well through that fog. Do not force her to make decisions through her panic with vague questions like "What do you need?" or "Is there anything I can do?" She doesn't know, and she wouldn't be able to tell you if she did. It's okay to make suggestions, like the one mentioned earlier about needing to go somewhere quiet, but always be specific, and the less the better. Don't bombard her with questions to make yourself feel better.

Additionally, do not force her into situations that she tells you are not good for her. Nica knows herself, how she is feeling, and whether she is at risk better than anyone, so respect those instincts. For example, if there is a large gathering that she feels she is not able to attend, do not push her into it. She is not making those choices to avoid commitments, she is making them because they are in her own best interest.

My supervisor's wariness proves sound. My friend goes to the bathroom in Dubai airport, where we are transiting, while we are waiting at the gate. We are called to go to the plane – and the anxiety of not knowing what to do brings on an attack. In the fog, I manage to get to my seat on the plane. But by the time my friend catches up with me, I have written out a note on the back of my boarding pass in trembling letters for the air hostess: can't speak or move my legs.

In South Africa, I have to travel from my home city of Cape Town to the city of Port Elizabeth[1], again with a friend who has kindly agreed to accompany and assist me. It turns out that, considering my condition and the funding I have for my fieldwork, the simplest way to get to my final location is to charter a long-distance Uber to the small town of Alice. It is still named for Princess Alice, the daughter of the British Queen Victoria, who never went there. I am in Alice to visit the archives known as the Repository of the Liberation Movement Archives held at the University of Fort Hare since 1992 – named for the nearby British fort that was built during their wars against the amaXhosa during the 19th century.

First built as the South African Native College in 1916, the college originated from the sometimes uneasy alliance between the new class of educated African Christians, supported by a number of traditional Southern African leaders, and early twentieth-century white liberals, many of them clergy. The religious tradition at the heart of Fort Hare's origin, shared by blacks and whites alike, heralded "plain living and high thinking", and a form of education that was undeniably Eurocentric. However, it did not make the assumption, central to the Bantu Education implemented in South Africa from the 1950s, that black Africans required or deserved a different, inferior education. Thus, the University of Fort Hare produced graduates from South Africa and as far north as Kenya and Uganda, who knew they were as good as the best. Many went on to prominent careers in fields as diverse as politics, medicine, literature and art (University of Fort Hare, 2025).

Alumni include many leaders of South Africa's anti-apartheid movement including Oliver Tambo, Govan Mbeki, Robert Sobukwe and Mangosuthu Buthelezi; African leading liberation figures including heads of state, such as Robert Mugabe and Herbert Chitepo of Zimbabwe; and Elius Mathu and Charles Njonjo of Kenya; and other black pioneers including the first black Zimbabwean medical doctor Tichafa Samuel Parirenyatwa and the first black woman medical doctor in South Africa, Dr Mary Maxakane. This last had particular resonance for me as the title of my study was *A Doctor Displaced: Nkosazana Dlamini Zuma in Exile 1976-1990.*

Working in the shadows of such history is astonishing – even if I have to sit on the floor of the documents room sometimes because my legs won't work.

We're sharing a room, something we've done many times before, but when I go into the bathroom it occurs to me not to latch the door for the first time. If I have an attack, he won't be able to get me out.

Nonetheless, thanks to the warmth of this friendship and the help of the head archivist Mosoabudi Mammoe, I am able to get on with my work.

6
Taxing travel: Ealing, London

Running shoes for stability. An A-line crimson coat from a charity shop for warmth against the English winter. Layers for shedding during panic attacks. A dodger blue hardshell plastic suitcase on wheels.

When is the worst of it?

I catch a bus, and then a train, and then another train, and halfway through the second train station, it happens. This is the difference between an anxiety disorder and a panic disorder (or so I've been informed). In an anxiety disorder, there's usually a trigger for a panic attack. And so, slowly but surely, you figure out what your triggers are and work around or even with them. Post-hospitalisation, I started to view my anxiety as a stern friend – she pulls that knowing face that I associate with my best friend when I am putting myself in a situation that isn't good for me, and then when I ignore her, she presses that small dingy white emergency button so that I can't ignore her anymore.

This is different. This is "I'm happily walking to class," one second and then, "That car is about to hit you, flee," the next. Nothing changes between the first and the second, except by the end of the second I'm chemically on the landing strip, ready for take-off.

It happens. I get onto the second train, somehow, after hanging up on my boyfriend mid-attack. By the time I call him back, I am dripping with sweat and wandering through a mall that isn't on my route to his home, refusing (loudly) to go straight to the flat, and telling him not to leave work to come and find me. People use the phrase "The world is spinning," but I've never really found it helpful. It's more like each unique fragment of the sensory world is politely and jovially waiting its turn to stab into the forehead area where yogis draw the third eye (does it count as your third when you can't see out of the two you already have?)

I insist I'll find a place to wait for him to finish work and go to a pub I remember having a friendly atmosphere. The first problem in this plan (apart from crossing roads mid-panic attack) is that it is late on a Friday. So, the pub is heaving with men. Once I get past this and find my way, dishevelled and damp, to a quiet corner I sink into the couch, strip off my layers, and realise…I've come to a pub.

At pubs, you have to order at the counter. Which is fine, except when you can't stand up. Having maxed out on adrenaline, my legs are on vacation. It is a long time before I can stand. By then, the pulsing masculinity of a London pub late Friday combines with my desperate humiliation at forgetting how to walk, and has me headed straight out the door.

And then, finally, I stumble into the fancy Italian restaurant Carluccios, in takkies and jeans, draped in the wet clothes I have shed, dragging luggage (literally and figuratively), struggling to see. And am welcomed.

Can I sit down? Of course!

Where is the bathroom? Downstairs, but why don't I use the staff one so I don't have to leave my bags too long…let's put them there where she can watch them for me…can she get me anything in the meantime?

I experience the kindness as oxygen.

And so, I return Friday after Friday, after the trauma of public transport mid-panic attack, as I wait for David to finish work.

There are spots of such kindness, inevitably. People are amazing. The departmental secretary does paperwork on my behalf and sends me cat pictures, after she finds me mid-attack one day and then learns that my cats help with my anxiety back home. The departmental supervisor comes to meet me in the bagel place across the road so I don't have to walk far. Friends take turns walking me to class when the noise and my shaking legs make getting there alone almost impossible.

I travel back to South Africa for primary research at the archive at Fort Hare University, a cradle of pan-Africanism. I am better at home – less attacks overall. It truly seems like my body is reacting to something about Oxford itself. I return to England, and then to the university for my third term. Before classes have even begun, my legs refuse to work again. On a call to my therapist back in South Africa, she insists I get proper help. I've gotten so used to it I timed my dissertation presentation precisely by how long I can stand. My lecturers, entertainingly, complimented me on its concision. I am bemused by my therapist's shock. "Something could be seriously wrong neurologically," she says. "Call someone for help. Now. While I am on the phone." I call the warden and am carted off for an emergency appointment with the GP. Third term hasn't begun but I've already racked up a medical emergency. The doctor says she can't find anything wrong. She recommends I go back to London, where I'll have someone keeping an eye on me. Somehow, I manage the train trip to Paddington, navigating that writhing nightmare of a station, and make it to Ealing. I have done the trip, while having panic attacks, so many times already – perhaps by now, it is just habit.

7
Moving in: Ealing, London

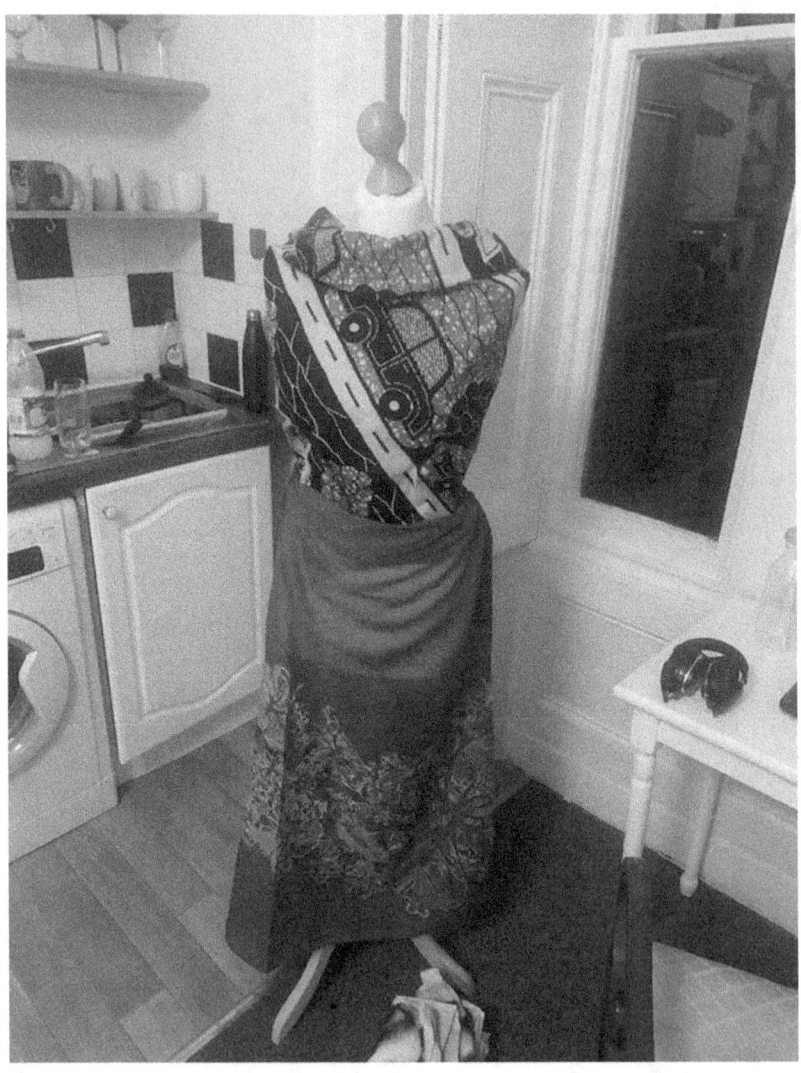

David orders a mannequin to make me feel more comfortable in the new flat. We name her Nicolette and take turns dressing her. She wears a sarong from home, and a cowl neck blouse shaped from Ankara I've had since I was 18 as a human rights volunteer in Accra, Ghana.

I find myself in a London flat that my boyfriend has just moved into. We've talked about me moving in one day, potentially, but not now, not like this. On my departmental supervisor's advice, I suspend my degree to save my life and just like that, we are living together.

The flat is nice enough, up a slightly crumbling set of white stairs to a slightly crumbling white exterior. One of those grand old houses surrounding Walpole Park in Ealing that evoke sensations of times gone by – people taking a turn in Walpole, women promenading along its paths. But now it is compartmented into multiple flats, owned by a company housed overseas. The landlord is a company name. Its plumbing needs work. The flat mostly consists of one tall, large room that serves as kitchen, dining room, lounge, and office. Luxuriously, one wall is almost wholly a window, looking out on a garden gone to seed. There is a separate bedroom, too small for a double bed, so there's a mattress on the floor instead. The door into it must either be jammed open behind the mattress or jammed almost shut so that I move horizontally through. The bathroom consists of a shower that routinely scalds me – it's the shock of this I hate the most. It tends to bring on a panic attack such that I am back in Oxford after a shower, lying naked, face down on the carpet in my student room, unable to sit up. A foreign child in an alien space in a foreign place.

I hang a cobalt blue fabric necklace from South African textile company African Baroque on the wall in the bathroom. It is the flat's only privacy when David is home and I need to make it more familiar somehow. Overall, the flat is not an unwelcoming space.

Rather it is apathetic to my presence. It was getting along fine with David alone, I am here now and surplus, flotsam washed up on its crumbling steps. There are tiny signs of me that I sent ahead – the wall of fairy-lights I ordered as a housewarming gift on Amazon from a bed in Cape Town, during my fieldwork back home. Tea and coffee containers I ordered on Etsy – a reminder of a happier time when I first visited David in his student digs in London and used our still slightly greasy curry containers (a treat for my very first night in England) to make tea and coffee containers for him. Homemade labels under Sellotape written in faint vermillion *koki* pen. Well, instant coffee. He had no tea. I had to brave the outside world to the Spar around the corner for a cup of tea – thank heavens the shop had the same name as a shop back home in South Africa. The range of teas certainly didn't. I was looking for Joko Five Roses. What the fuck was PG Tips?

But here, we'd moved up in the world, down the road from that tiny, long student digs where I'd first played at homemaking for us. I'd picked flowers off a field at the side of the road. I'd bought beautiful, smooth nectarines to make a fruit bowl. I'd played at making his room comfortable then panicked – what if he hated the presumption of it? I thought I was interfering, overplaying my hand as a long-distance girlfriend. We'd only known each other three months in South Africa, despite our families' shared history, before he'd left for exotic, rich London. I may have worked multiple jobs to visit him but what did I know? But he'd come home and sputtered with joy. Told all his cool film school friends at the pub that night, how much better I'd made coming home from university. They'd smiled indulgently and there'd been such possibility in the muggy London night that I'd thought I might be set alight by it.

Now there was furniture we owned in a flat with two rooms instead of one, but so much less hope. Here is my next attempt at homemaking, a list of the things we need – more forks, a bathmat *ensovoorts* (and so on in Afrikaans). But I am a shambles of that girl and I believe that he has no notion what he has taken on just by loving me.

8
A porcelain pillbox: Ealing, London

The beautiful New Look red court shoes made of a lovely candy apple red suede. They remind me of the shoes and accessories section of the sell-out Victoria & Albert featured exhibition Dior: Designer of Dreams. Their sublime silhouette makes me feel as though I should be twirling in a piece from his New Look collection, with its luxurious layers of skirt. Unfortunately, walking in them is a different matter entirely as they are a size too small! But the sight of them brings me such joy so they pay their way as bookends. Having one of a pair on each end of the shelf makes for a tidy and elegant sight.

We're spring cleaning, and that included clearing out the medicine box.

I don't know if this is what they had in mind with the term "flushing your drugs", but it's what I find myself doing on a Saturday afternoon to ensure no-one ends up on intense psychiatric drugs they shouldn't be taking. This caution is experience-based. A few weeks ago, a doctor took me off diazepam – telling me I shouldn't have been put on it in the first place, let alone kept on it for so long. She didn't take me off it slowly, a process known as weaning (a word only regularly used in the context of babies). She told me to stop taking it, and the door label said she was a doctor, so I did (Googling medication you've been put on does not help with an anxiety disorder).

The escalation of my symptoms was so severe that I found myself having a depressive episode for the first time in two years. This culminated in sobbing on a park bench. (This appears elegant in Adele music videos. In reality, not so much.) I'd fled the house because suicide ideation (doctors/counsellors/therapists/nurses/welfare officers are always impressed when you use this terminology) had come to give me a flat-warming present.

At an emergency appointment the next day, the other doctor (his name was also on his door) informed me that the drug I'd been on is considered highly addictive – so what I was experiencing was a major drug withdrawal, for which people were usually hospitalised.

People spend a lot of time talking about the importance of asking for help. They are utterly and completely right. But the other part of the equation is as important, if not more so. People actually have to give it. I've been telling people with more qualifications than me that I'm in trouble for eight months. And I'm still waiting for one of them to actually you know…help.

Anyway, despite Friday's three phone consultations with medical professionals, this hasn't happened. But, in stylistic news, I've found a way to feel slightly less despairing about having to take pills multiple times a day, never knowing if they are a good idea or just making the problem worse (as it turns out the 'tranquilizers' I've been on for four months have been doing).

The idea of a pillbox is an old-fashioned one. But when you have to take as many pills as I do, it can genuinely help.

The first of these was picked up on my first Christmas trip to London. It's small, dainty and pretty – oval and porcelain, with a rose floral pattern painted on its lid. This is just what I need. Each time I open it, I feel like the eight-year-old on my mom's friend who was a wardrobe mistress's bed, unpacking all her incredible jewellery, treating each piece as a horse that might startle, and glorying in the faded velvet and luscious satin of her proper old jewellery boxes. They were precisely that to me – jewels. I remember the extravagantly glamorous woman who sold it to me for half the price because it was Christmas, and I think of all the women it may have known. And it hurts just a little less that I have to put the tight red capsule on my tongue within 30 minutes of waking.

As the detective in the TV show *Death in Paradise* says, "There's little enough happiness in the world. When it comes your way, you got to grab it with both hands."

9
Exotic Ealing: Ealing, London

A long loose cornflower blue dress with white polka dots, made for summer holidays or maternity. Or illness, apparently.

Travelling as a South African, there are a lot of assumptions made about animals. I try not to mention my uncle who is an animal wrangler for movies and as such has lions, cheetahs, giraffes, and hyenas on his farm. People don't need encouragement to do the whole exotify Africa thing – they do it all on their own.

London has to be the most exotic city I've ever lived in. Cape Town had zebra and wildebeest that grazed on the slopes of Table Mountain, which I saw on the way to school. But it was home. Accra had goats, which are common. And even if they weren't, no-one who has ever met a goat thinks it's "foreign, tropical, unnaturalized, alien" or any of the other weird, xenophobia-embedded, coded words the dictionary provides in its bid to define "exotic."

Foxes on the other hand…every time I see the fox who beds down in our garden, I hold my breath. It slinks over our neighbour's wall, and under our picnic table to disappear into the crisp green foliage. I am nine, winning a competition for writing about how Fantastic Mr Fox could have escaped the burrow alone but stayed with his family in danger instead.

In my London flat, there's a bumblebee that flies through the window that is too heavy for me to open properly. It's so dense you wouldn't imagine it could get off the ground. Then, there's the fly I've named Geoffrey to try to make him less annoying.

You see, I can't move my legs. The phrasing of that sentence is interesting – like I am somehow separate from my legs. They're unruly. It's like giving orders to a cat. The Duke of Cambridge, as part of the well-intended attempt to tackle mental health stigma, earlier this year described how "If you have a broken leg, then you go and see the doctor. You wouldn't turn around and say, 'I can manage this' with an open fracture." It's a common enough comparison, and he's right, of course. But I worry that this separation creates an illusion about how physical mental health can be. As I told the woman during the fourth of my five medical appointments in two weeks today, I don't have any long-standing physical health conditions. In that sense, I'm a relatively healthy young woman – although heavier and weaker than I used to be thanks to not being able to walk around the block alone for months. But today, I can't move my legs.

In today's appointment, I was asked if I am managing everyday tasks like washing (a friend's tip is that you can get away with Febreze air freshener for two weeks at a time). Washing requires standing, which I can do, but only most of the time.

When I'm asked to list my symptoms for what must be the 459 672nd time, I don't talk about feelings. It goes like this: fatigue, shaking, sweating, hot flushes, immobility, difficulty speaking.

Oh, that's my favourite. Speech was my last line of defence – even when you have to go down on your knees in an elevator full of strangers, or crawl up the stairs, you can still be wry or sly, make 'em laugh. As Paolo Nutini sings in *Iron Sky*, "We are proud individuals living on the city, but the flames couldn't go much higher…"

Now that is slipping. So, here I am, with Geoffrey, Big-Ass Bumblebee, and the Fox for companions. Nutini's next line is, "We find gods and religions to paint us with salvation." But the local church is locked and requires walking.

10
Five roses: Ealing, London

> *A watermelon pink crocheted shawl that I made when hospitalised for depression before coming to England, draped on a tough navy blue couch too little for lounging.*

David brings me flowers just to make me smile.

These five immaculate pink roses are finally surviving on the bathroom windowsill. I place them in an olive jar, which still has its labels. I like the contrast – something so pristine as a pale pink rose that hasn't shed a single petal, displayed in something practically clunky with a list of ingredients on the side.

Want to settle into a new place? Be forced to remain there 23 hours a day, seven days a week for weeks in a row. It's not the scenario in which I imagined 'moving in together' would happen when I saw it on television.

I like the sound of the birds that reach me from the communal garden; the slightly off angle of the front left leg of the desk we found in a charity shop; the only light in our bedroom being fairy lights.

I don't like that I still wait for my boyfriend to get home so he can take the rubbish out, for fear of leaving the flat alone; I don't have the strength to do the dishes in one sitting; I can't lift the laundry rack or open the window properly; Geoffrey the Fly is thrilled to test the patience of the patient.

I practise going to the park. I can only go for a few minutes at a time and not every day. But if I make it across the road, that's progress for me. The doctor has put me on the waiting list to see a psychiatrist. I have tried every other route I can find for help online – I've done phone interviews for various mental health services. I am on the waiting list for Cognitive Behavioural Therapy too. It's the one thing my South African therapist I no longer see said I should avoid having, but it's all they have on offer.

The interviews are hard because I can't always speak, especially not to a stranger about medical details. They send me a letter each time to tell me the whole story in writing, by way of rejection. So, at least I have a written record of why I can't access help.

The image of mental illness I have in my head (unintentional mental illness pun) is an old postcard, internalised somewhere along the way. A white woman in a sepia-tinted black and white photograph with hair she definitely didn't do herself; an Erdem-style dress (frills, ruffles, florals, excess fabric); the tips of pinching black boots showing. One almost can't imagine her having skin. She is wan.

Perhaps this is why I clawed my way back to life in a psychiatric ward via colour. I started colouring in and it spilled out of me. The nurses started coming in to see the new one that I stuck up on the wall each day. When I was discharged, they came with me, and went up on my wall at home. And were soon joined by new ones, until there was more colour than wall.

With a colouring of a Thomas Kinkade, known as the Painter of Light, the wall in my tenth home since I was 18 has just begun. And these five roses are alive today.

11
Walking in Walpole: Ealing, London

Block heel boots, clunky with confidence.

Today, it's the fatigue that is overwhelming.

I can't quite sleep, nor can I keep my eyes open, unlike our new cat whose eyes are like the reverse of CDs in her hiding place beneath the couch.

I managed a brisk walk around the park this morning and have been horizontal since. I could have done it in jeans and a T-shirt. But clothing has always been inextricable from context, for me. Since it is the most exercise of which I have been capable in a while, I needed to wear exercise clothes to feel like it 'counted' as progress.

I couldn't wear the block heel boots that normally give me confidence to the emergency doctor's appointment last week. I tried to put them on, but some days my balance is off, and I need to move carefully down the eight peeling white steps that lead up to our building.

12
Alone and unsafe: Ealing, London

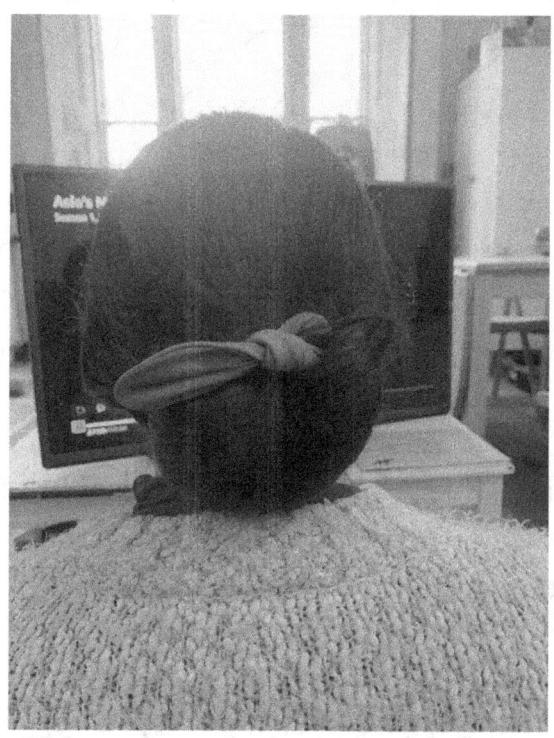

A blue bun maker, bought off newly discovered Etsy at the expensive price of £6.99, worn with a bulky cream jersey from a charity shop.

The cat is old. She is already 15 years old. In cat years, that's ancient. But for an old cat, there is little wrong with her. She is an indoor cat, they tell us. That is a vaguely strange concept to me but necessary since we didn't live on the ground floor. She's a calico, missing a part of one eyelid and multiple teeth. She starts coming out from under the too firm and dull blue couch, but she still hides if one of us moves too fast, speaks too loudly or does…pretty much anything. I am okay with it. I know the feeling. Her company helps me – having a living creature in the flat that isn't me.

David has to go away and we go around in circles about it for days. His family has a long-planned holiday in Portugal. His parents have been counting down. But I am to be left alone in the flat – and all I can think is, what if I have an attack? Cannot move and he isn't in calling distance. It's tough enough in the day when he is at work around the corner at the film school. Some part of me knows he is entirely in the right – he can't have to be here all the time. It can't be this big a deal that he's going away for a week. But it is. It goddamn is and that is not my fault either. I am not well enough to sublimate my needs. All I can think is how dangerous it is going to be for me to be alone. So finally, he tells his parents he's going to go for less time and his mother tells him he's driving a knife through her heart. He is torn and all I can see is him putting me on a train to Oxford mid-panic attack again, sending me away when I cannot trust my own body. But this is worse than being sent away somehow. This is being left, with all the echoes of a little girl whose dad walked out long ago. I want to be understanding and adult, but I am not. I am nine years old and hiding in the cupboard.

Eventually we stock the fridge, so I won't have to face the shops. I've not done so alone in months. We install a panic button on my phone; and I press it too soon after he left. He thought it would signal an emergency. Everything is an emergency to me. We ensure a friend of his from work knows I'm alone and may call for help if something happens. This is how we manage a four-day trip when I am 26.

13
Mary's Living & Giving: Ealing, London

A crocheted blanket of various pinks, purples and whites – granny squares sewn together. I made it in my Honours year, studying Political and International Studies and stitching myself together, one lopsided and holey square at a time.

I spend my days, and scholarship money, watching *Midsomer Murders*, ironically, to feel safe. I recall afternoons watching it under duvets with my million cousins, while it rained outside. Those were my grandmother's videotaped recordings.

We walk past a sign that says the fancy looking charity shop that raises money for Save the Children down the road is looking for a volunteer to run their social media. I've run Twitter for the Africa Matters Initiative, have Instagram, and love clothes. My mind, in the moments when it is clear, when I'm not weeping or sweating or trembling, is eating itself from boredom. Mary's Living and Giving on Ealing Green is a boutique. I've been in once but was too intimidated by its chicly colour-coded rails and warm lighting. I buy clothes from charity shops with bargain bins. But here they are asking for a volunteer, and I'll only have to cross one road.

I sit with nerves dancing in my stomach, downstairs at the shop. I've completed the online application. It's now a question of an interview. Sandhya comes barrelling down the stairs to meet me. She is wearing hot pink lipstick, a leather jacket, and black platform heels. She is also shorter than me, in striking contrast to David's towering frame. I've prepared a plan based on the other Mary's Living & Giving Instagram accounts and have an idea for a local campaign celebrating local sights and landmarks in photoshoots highlighting the shop's chic second-hand items. She says, "Go ahead." "I'm quite ill so sometimes I'll have to unpredictably cancel or move things. I have these attacks, you see…" She doesn't blink. "So, we'll cancel and move things." Something clicks into place for the first time in Ealing.

14
Calleycat the alleycat: Ealing, London

David's long black puffer jacket, worn over a satin champagne nightgown, with no socks and old pale grey takkies.

I've already been weeping when the indoor emotional support cat, recognising a lost cause when she sees one, decides it is time to become an outdoor cat.

She's not actually great at emotional support. I mean, if she could talk, we could probably compare PTSD. As it is, she changes her mind mid-stroke about whether she wants to be stroked and she's jumpier than me. David drops a dish – the cat and I are both in the other room, quivering. She's also lopsided, so her backside knocks things over without her front end realising – inducing major panic regularly. She has the temperament of that old guy in the pub (see, I'm learning British things?). Things make her angry that have been there all along. She wakes up on a Thursday and finds the chair suspicious, so she hisses at it. She rolls over on a Monday and the colouring book has become a source of ire. The Wednesday before last, she made it clear that that tail of hers is a traitor.

But you know, she's company in a foreign place when I can't go out much or you know, talk to people. She cuddles next to me on the couch, takes up residence on our bed, and stroking her, or listening to her small shuffling snore, stabilises my breathing.

And now she's run away, taking our peace of mind along with her. She has a bell around her neck. Do you know how many everyday sounds could be a bell? Your keys are jangling, you dropped some coins. Suddenly, for the first time I consider saying yes when the mental health nurse asks, "Are you hearing things?"

It's been just over a week. We've done everything we, the charity, the neighbour, our moms, and the internet, can think of. So now I do the work of trying to accept she might not want to live with us anymore (you can't force a cat to do jack) and try to be mature and think maybe she came to me when I really needed her and that's all. But each day, there's a moment when I hold a small breath, hoping the phone is ringing because someone has seen our poster and knows where she is.

We have had every door and window open for days in case she returns. The neighbours are great about it – even letting me know via WhatsApp when they see her nearby. But exposing the flat to the world in this way shatters any crust of safety I have cultivated here. Our mothers have started to say, "She'll return if she wants to," trying to ease the blow. But it is the one thing we had to look after together that was not my illness with too many names. She is small and fluffy and old, and we'd given her a home. This home, such as it is, with an IKEA wooden table and a crate we found on the street on the way home from the doctor. This home that was already shuddering with all it was holding was a safe place for at least one thing – the cat who is now gone. We hear her bell every now and then and run out in the middle of the night.

One night, I hear her and grab the one winter puffer jacket we own, slamming it on over a pale satin nightgown I once wore in the hospital and shoving my feet into takkies I used to wear for RunWalkForLife in Cape Town suburbia before I came to this wretched country. David comes out but he's been drinking so isn't fully conscious. I tell him I'm going searching in the garden next door, further than I go even in the daytime usually. He turns around and walks back inside.

Another night, I hear her when I'm on watch. Quickly, I am outside in the plastering rain and a flash of lightning reveals her seated on the left wall of the garden outside. I do not think I am so afraid we will lose her again, this scruffy symbol of our attempt to make a life midst the waves that are crashing upon us. I simply grab her without any aim. She scuffles and slides on my wet puffy jacket until, in fear, she sinks one of her few leftover teeth into my hand. I try not to let go but can't hold on. She is gone.

The next day, my hand is turning red, and the internet says cat bites require treatment. The doctors' is closed as it is the weekend so it's an Uber to A&E. Nowadays, I loathe anything medical, feeling by this stage that they are actively trying to kill me by negligence or direct malice. I have no faith in the world-famous NHS. We ask friends of David's to wait at the flat in case Calley, who we have taken to calling the Bean because of the shape she lies in, returns. We spend six hours in the A&E. As ever, David is at my side the whole time as I grow more and more panicky. I am wearing the noise-cancelling headphones he bought online. They've made walks around the block possible.

We pass the time as two former Drama students – imagining a script of the players in the emergency room, the young brown boy translating for his mum, the *gatvol* nurses, the various injuries that drift in barefoot. We almost don't make it. I am replete with tension when the doctor finally sees me. He gives me antibiotics and sends me for an X-ray. I've paid the health surcharge to access the NHS but thus far it's brought nothing but grief. This day, I am amazed when no one demands my student card, Biometric Residence Permit or even wallet, that I'd scrambled from the bottom drawer of my desk. Something in me softens, slightly, towards the medical professionals I've begun to view with such acute suspicion for their general lack of care.

The cat returns on David's watch. We've gotten a full-blown trap from the woman who fostered the Bean previously and laid on particularly smelly wet cat food knowing that she will be hungry by now. It's 10 days in and we've only gotten more desperate, not less. David wakes me to show me the small, scared creature in our living room. I've become afraid we're now trapping her here for good. Surely if she wants to be outside, we should let her? But this time, we open the trap and she bolts out, much skinnier than before. Upon finding herself in familiar surroundings, she flops relaxedly to the floor. She is home. We have made a home.

15
Medication: Ealing, London

A lurid pink and purple, striped poncho, worn with black Ug-boots for warmth in the South African town of McGregor at the foot of Riviersonderend (River without end in Afrikaans) mountains.

I remember the first time I put a psychotropic drug into my body. I was 18. They'd wanted to prescribe them for my depression for years. I refused. At least that way, I knew that whatever I was experiencing, it was me. I don't really know how to communicate this now, with the bevy of drugs they have had me on since. You'd think it wouldn't make a difference. Surely, as long as you+medication feels better, then there is some of you that feels better?

The terrible truth is that they cannot guarantee if/when you will feel better. When the medication is right, it's miraculous. I was in hospital when they got mine right the first time, and there was a significant improvement in 24 hours. I quite literally sat up straighter.

But I was 23 when that happened. There were five years in between – two degrees, one relationship, approximately 1,825 days of my life, when they hadn't got it right. That's five years of the depression + side effects + weaning + withdrawal +

changing medication + new side effects + getting off for a while + depression.

I hate that word, 'side effects.' It connotes things that happen on the side, like a sauce that is optional. It's not optional, nor on the side, if it affects every day. It shaped my first experiences of sex, travelling alone, university, and adult life.

This year, the physical side effects of the drug they put me on to help manage my panic disorder included overwhelming fatigue, shaking, weakness, sweating, hot flushes, and dissociation (all of which are also symptoms of a panic disorder). The life effects of those side effects included hearing that I might have some kind of neurological problem, countless doctors' appointments, having to prepare my friends and family for how to care for me, almost being killed in a car accident, being rescued by a stranger, being lifted and dressed by my boyfriend, suspending my master's degree, and as finally burst out of me mid-sob the other night, a deep rooted fear that I was about to die.

You see, knowing matters. Knowing it was the pills that caused the most extreme and unknown of my physical symptoms, which we now do, helps. It helps me to know that I'm not going mad – my body is not simply coming apart. I am not dying.

I'm off those particular pills now. But the life effects don't stop with the side effects. It is almost impossible to disentangle what was the panic disorder and what was the medication I was given to manage it. Now, all else must be paused as I seek treatment for the panic disorder – and rest and recovery for the shitstorm that came with its medical mismanagement.

Finding the right medication in June 2016 saved my life. Being on the wrong ones before that deformed it. Being put on the wrong ones this year almost destroyed it.

So, I go back and watch my 18-year-old self on holiday with her best friend, feverishly reading *The Secret Magdalene* for the first time, eating apple crumble with double cream Greek yoghurt, and kneading the thought of the unopened box of pills in the folds of her bag.

I watch her sit on the cold cement bench in her mom's lurid pink and purple striped textured poncho, watching the ducks square off in the winter sun. I watch her go inside the thatch-roof cottage, open the box and place one tablet on her tongue.

And suddenly, I am relieved I cannot go back to tell her to do anything differently. I just don't know what I'd tell her.

16 Medical illness: Ealing, London

A duck blue T-shirt, worn with Primark skinny jeans, and a tasselled royal blue shawl around my hips.

It's like trying to explain peanut butter.

My ex-boyfriend was allergic to peanuts, so he's never eaten the stuff. I used to try and wrap my brain around that concept. It's not that I can't comprehend someone not liking it. It was not having ever known the taste of it that I simply can't grasp. It's such a distinct experience, that peculiar mix of sweet and savoury tastes gumming one's mouth together. It simply cannot be communicated via description. It's sensory.

It can be like that, trying to relay what it is like to live with mental illness.

In the past 9 months, I have spoken to a clinical psychologist, Cognitive Behavioural therapists, General Practitioners, receptionists, administrators, a psychiatrist, lecturers, friends, a boyfriend, supervisors, strangers on a train, a priest, a judge, family, a mental health nurse, three members of the college welfare team, academic registrars, a disability advisor, and a cat, about my mental health crisis. I'll give you three guesses who helped the most (it's not the ones who specialise in the stuff).

Before I had to suspend my studies because no-one seemed entirely sure whether my body was just running out of steam (the technical jargon for this is adrenal fatigue) after eight months of daily panic attacks or I had some undiagnosed lurking menace of a brain disease, I kept a diagram of all the people I had to speak to about my health. Those patronising classes on how to use flow-charts to help with your studies came in useful after all. Right up until I left, there was a woman being CCed in all the university's emails about my health (with information it took me years to tell my best friends) who had never contacted me directly. Apparently, she was my department's disability liaison, for all my needs as a student with a registered disability.

So, first, communicating what it is like is brutally hard, even in the best of circumstances – even when it's your beloved partner, and you're lying under the covers in a sanctuary of safety and support. Even then – it's excruciating. So, imagine what it is like to talk to a bunch of bloody strangers in a foreign country who just ask you if you're suicidal so often that if you weren't at the beginning of the conversation…and then tell you to call 999, if you are.

Second, the administration of talking to that many people, of not being helped, of trying to find another person who maybe can, and going over it all again is toxically tiring. Today and yesterday, I've barely been able to keep my eyes open. I had to take a break to lie down halfway through hanging the washing. I'm gummed up with the peanut butter of it all, the thick, sticky, smothering task of being the personal assistant to my disease.

At the beginning of this year, the precise beginning, I sat with a group of people at a party in London. Everyone was saying a New Year's resolution. It got to me, I said, "Don't die." Everyone chuckled, in the delirium of champagne and fancy dress, I suppose it sounded funny to them. I wasn't trying to be funny. I wasn't even being pessimistic. I was just being honest.

How do you communicate that?

17
Don't lock the door: Ealing, London

A black cotton V-neck blouse, with white polka dots, worn with navy blue skinny jeans and pale grey takkies.

The cat is home which is sublime. She's still a crappy emotional support animal, but I significantly prefer it when she is one in residence. It's been me and her for the past few days, as David is working. She mostly sleeps. But the small shuffling noises she makes as she does so help with the oddity of a life lived in isolation.

Part II

18
Elegance in Ealing: Ealing, London

A blue and green ASOS rose print sleeveless dress with a full-length zip and stud collar, worn with blue suede Autograph heels; a ruched Gina Bacconi animal long sleeve dress; and green Zara dress with a dust ruffle hem. These are the outfits I wear for the photoshoot at Mooch Ealing.

We find a good doctor. He hasn't said or done anything groundbreaking. He just isn't being shit, which at this point feels like such a miracle that I thank him for it at the end of our first appointment. It takes me some time to get the words out of my mouth but I get there eventually.

I do my first posts on Mary's Living and Giving Instagram – a pointed black and white pair of Ernesto Esposito shoes, followed by a Tommy Hilfiger dress. In the shop, I feast on snippets of elegance. I can't do the normal volunteering shifts. I do one and barely make it home. Two hours is simply too long for me to be on my feet. But I can snap photographs of beautiful garments and accessories on my phone and sometimes, when I have the energy, I sit quietly in the basement and use my researching skills to help price items.

I organise our first photoshoot.

First, the friend who we warned I was alone when David went to Portugal agrees to model.

I meet her at the shop to try on a few things I've selected. I discover I can access a taste of the feeling I used to get from dressing up – by dressing someone else.

Each of these acts is revolutionary for me. Stepping beyond the flat. I go to fetch the clothes on the day of the photoshoot. I greet the other volunteers at the shop nervously when I anxiously tell them, I've come to collect some clothes for a photoshoot. I'm already sweating. But maybe Sandhya has warned them. They treat it as a non-event, and let me leave with £100 of merchandise. This is a vast amount to me, something like R2000 back home, and I'm somewhat overwhelmed at the responsibility. But this unblinking trust is also filling me up, at a time when trusting my own legs to work is still tough.

My world mainly consists of the flat and the park – so I ask her to pose in the park, with the option of running back to the flat in between looks for her to get changed. David has agreed to play photographer, as he works in film and has a good camera. I've been so busy preparing that I only realise when I'm crossing the road to the park that I'm wearing shorts. I haven't shown this much of my body in public since I left for Oxford, but on this day I have somewhere to be so after a quick glance down at my thighs I charge ahead to the park. I am intimidated by the fact that she has modelled professionally before – and they both work in film. They must know more than me about how to conduct a photoshoot. But they're looking to me on this one, and this is Walpole

Park – almost the only place in the world I go. I know where I am in Walpole. I know it by smell. Once we've done the first series of photos, of her in a striking, black Phase Eight evening gown with cut outs at the waist standing in the greenery, I start to discover that I actually have quite a clear vision of what I want. I ask her to pose midst the spring flowers to match the floral print of her Jasper Conran dress. I manage to make her laugh and David captures her spinning, the silhouette of the skirt swinging in motion.

There is something whimsical about the vintage silk CC dress with beaded roses she wears next, so I pose her beneath the arch around which flowers and vines grow near Pitzhanger Manor. This whole park used to be its private garden. Finally, she is thoroughly modern in an emerald-green Phase Eight jumpsuit with yellow suede block heels, and sunglasses. I seat her on a graffitied wooden bench. We're done and I am elated. I post a sneak peek on our Instagram account – describing it as the first of our new series of photoshoots celebrating, "Ealing sites, businesses and talent." I want to thank our friend for modelling so with her permission I tag her, and David for the photography, crediting myself with styling. It feels weird but is also…invigorating. I break up the shoot into outfits, so I can highlight each look in a post. When I share our first full look, I describe our setting of Walpole Park as "a magnificent park where Ealing residents stroll, jog, picnic, play and wonder." I come up with a name for this new endeavour – Elegance in Ealing.

Next, we go to our second favourite place in Ealing. Once a week for a month or two, we've gone to the Cheddar Deli to purchase a small amount of cheese. I look forward to it all week. My one adventure. I can do the walk only because David is with me. But for a little while each week, it's been true that we're just a young couple who enjoy eating and playing at podcasting about cheese. We pretend that we're fancy and know sophisticated words about gastronomy. I contact them, and they are happy to be our first business to enjoy the free publicity. It is now July so I select summer dresses for the young volunteer from the shop who is happy to pose for us midst giant wheels of cheese – a Banana Republic cowl necked pink number; a structured Tara Jarmon vermillion dress with a ruffled bodice; and a flowing Oasis floral dress paired with purple Tod's slingback heels. She is from Serbia and enjoys telling the proprietor about the cheeses back home. I am reminded for a few seconds that I belong to a community of foreigners in London – I am not alone in my otherness.

I'm still posting about other local happenings and pieces of shop news midst the new Elegance in Ealing photoshoots, but it is these posts that receive an overwhelmingly positive response. People like seeing beauty in the places they know.

We visit Sandhya's favourite local coffee shop, the Moon & Maybe. I style her in a red satin cocktail dress from JAX that shows off her figure, and she twirls in a black chiffon Zara blouse with a patterned and pleated leather skirt from Gracia Fashion. Finally, she fans herself with a peach feathered fan, wearing a vintage dusky pale pink Parigi dress with a neck sash, white floral detailing, and three buttons on the left shoulder. She tells me I have an eye for this – selecting pieces that look excellent on someone, that they'd never think to wear. I beam. It's so long since I have felt skilled at anything.

After the shoot, we sit and drink cappuccinos and eat a peanut butter brownie – talking, just talking normally. We talk about our families and what's been happening lately. I still have to sit with my back to the wall in the outside space, but I can do this now, sit in a coffee shop and feel – just for a few moments – like a whole human being.

There are chinks of light. I have a cat and a campaign.

19
Foreign fiancée: Ealing, London

A baby blue loose cotton patterned shirt, reminiscent of a dashiki. I wear it as a dress in the flat, for the heat of London.

The message comes from Oxford: because I suspended my degree, the Home Office is going to revoke my student visa. Any sense of the earth firming beneath my feet is eviscerated.

I use all my academic research skills and still the only answer available to us is: get married.

At first, we discuss a civil partnership because that seems less momentous and overwhelming somehow for a young couple already dealing with a significant health crisis, but the new legislation giving access to heterosexual couples hasn't made its way through Parliament yet. We need to make a plan sooner than that. I'm pitching marriage to my boyfriend, two months after moving in together, six months after moving to the country, after a year and a half of long distance. This is a terrible idea.

But if I leave, I'll never resume my degree. The whole point is to stabilise and assimilate here enough to be well enough to do so. And, despite the shitshow we've been star players in, we know we want to be together. If anything, the fact that we *still* want to be together after what we've gone through is testimony to that. So, marriage it is. At first, we say we're getting married but *not really*. It'll just be a piece of paper and we'll pretend we're still just us. Our parents are, to say the least, sceptical but there's a surprising lack of resistance. Maybe we just sound too tired to be fought with. But I know his mom has phoned my mom to ask what she thinks. We go back and forth. Finally, once we've decided we'll do it but be sure to name it anything but, I'm sitting on our mattress bed when he comes home from the pub after too many pints.

I've just spent two hours on a WhatsApp phone call with one of my best friends back home. We're on JJ's House fashion website looking for a dress for me to marry in. I know it can't be white. I'm saving that for the wedding day which, I keep insisting, *this is not*. But I want something special, something light and flowing, that disguises this much bigger body I have as a result of being unable to move or cook for months. I've just chosen a dress – the first time I've ordered something new online for myself ever. It's on a sample sale, at a third of the price, but at £60 including postage is still more than I've spent on a dress for myself before. It's taken all my friend's encouragement to buy it. David comes in, and announces dramatically, "Let's just get married." I'm secretly glad, although also terrified. My parents never married and my dad left. I don't exactly have a model for how this works or what this means. But that's the plan. I'm 26, in a foreign country, frequently so sick I can't stand or speak, but we're getting married.

20
Engaged: Ealing, London

A white spaghetti strap top printed with butterflies, worn with a red ZARA cardigan from a charity shop.

We file the papers in Haringey because I like their principles. They're the only registrar's office that publicly acknowledges its duty to provide the cheapest package available for couples getting married. We've never been to Haringey before this. The travel is tough as always. We don't leave Ealing much. Not just because of me. David has a perimeter he doesn't particularly like to go beyond. He's happy with work, the shops, the flat and the pub. Thank God, because I can only manage the flat, the charity shop and the park. Although I'd have liked the symbolism, Ealing is far out of our price range even at their cheapest – it's all built in with a venue you have to pay for *ensovoorts* (and so on in Afrikaans). We've made the phone calls, telling my extended family I'm now officially engaged. I've asked my aunt to send photographs of my granny's ring as inspiration.

I find out David has sweetly gone ahead and ordered a ring on a whim on Etsy. Miraculously, it looks a lot like my granny's. It's a bit too big – but the wedding band I've ordered will keep it on. I've gotten the campaign into local newsletters. I'm comfortable at the shop, enjoying styling people and getting to know the area. We're getting more followers on the accounts, and most importantly more volunteers and donations from people who are crediting the campaign.

21
Stuttering shame: Ealing, London

A lime green T-shirt, worn with a maxi skirt printed in blues and greens. A red leather handbag David bought for me for Christmas.

I want today to be good, for it to be within my power to make it so. It isn't.

One of the symptoms that had to be confirmed as panic-associated, and brought about broader concerns, is that when I have a bad enough attack, I can struggle to talk for a while afterwards. It's like the words get clogged in my oesophagus. By the time I get them past throat, tongue, teeth, they're a little mangled. I stutter. I stutter and I burn with mortification.

I sit in the bizarre waiting room, full of people who all face one way and don't speak to each other, and I drip. I've always sweated easily, and always been shy about it. Along the way to becoming a grown-up woman, some convergence of voices tells you that you are not supposed to try. If you do anything other than sit merging with the wallpaper, you're not supposed to show signs of effort. It's why I like watching Etta James sing *At Last* live at Montreux in 1975 – she sweats with the effort of it. I wrote and published a whole academic paper about it, this monstrous management of the self that women are disciplined into. It was entitled *Kate Middleton and White Femininity: Excess Transgresses*. I wrote it for my Gender course in my Honours year in 2015, studying Political and International Studies at Rhodes University, and then published it in *Africa, UK & Ireland: Writing Politics and Knowledge Production* in 2018.

And still, I can't shake this shit. Since the panic disorder ascended from somewhere in the bowels of my childhood, the sweating is near constant. I sit in the nice doctor man's waiting room, post-panic attack, and each lingering drop of slippery stickiness blazes a trail of my shame.

I can't control my voice. I can't control my brain which constantly sends SOS messages to my central nervous system, even when you know…it's entirely fucking unnecessary. And now and then, I still can't control my limbs. For months, the adrenal fatigue and panic attacks have ravaged me. I've therefore also lost the taut control I've had on my weight for a decade. And so, the merry-go-round of my eating disorder days has begun chugging fuel like tequila again.

So, today, I try to do the mature thing and start figuring out how to dress this new body instead of just hating it, with all its out-of-nowhere stretchmarks that I only spotted recently. Seven and a half minutes in the changing room does not transform me into a new, confident self. It transforms me into an almost-crying, bra-less, sweating girl who can't walk home.

Today is not good. Maybe tomorrow.

22
Paperwork purgatory: Ealing, London

A full-length dashiki-style, bright red dress, worn loose and bought on the streets of Accra, Ghana.

Do you know what made today hard? A fly.

I was trying to do the washing up, like a grown-up. There is a lot of it to be done – all of it really. There is now not a single clean thing to drink from in the house. Unless you count bowls. There are three clean bowls, as of this morning when I had yoghurt and fruit. Did I mention that is all I have eaten today? The commonly spouted wisdom is that four to five portions of fruit/vegetables a day keep the doctor away. I mean, in my case, they don't, but I'm different. I have many pieces of paper saying so.

It's hard, putting it on paper. In the UK, a long-term mental illness such as mine is legally recognised as a disability under the Equality Act, in that it "has a substantial, adverse, and long-term effect" on my capacity to function on a day-to-day basis. So, I sucked up the fear of stigma, and the inner voices that constantly tell you that mental illness doesn't really count as a disability, and the part of me that is so determined not to be defined by it etc. and ticked the box on the 8762 forms that I filled out before coming here to study. I registered with the Disability Advisory Service at Oxford University and was deeply reassured that they seemed proactive and engaged.

So basically, I was fooled by the pieces of paper, with their fancy titles like 'Disability Liaison.' The systems, and people, I came into contact with had no fucking clue.

Some people were kind. There are always some kind people to be found wherever you are. But these were not the people with the titles, and supposedly qualifications, and pay cheques, for helping me. These were just people who move in the world with kindness, who see a girl in the middle of a road, dripping with sweat and shaking, and walk her across. The classmate you barely know who gets down on his knees next to you where you have fallen on your first day of class and helps you find the beta blockers in your bag; the new friend who doesn't make a big deal out of it when you need to be walked home to make sure you don't collapse. These people are kind, and probably saved my life.

But that is the problem. My life should not have been in danger, in the first place.

When I got on the plane to come here, my psychiatrist considered my depression and anxiety to be "in remission." His words. No doubt, all of the change would have been difficult for anyone, and for someone with my diagnosis and history, a risk. But I had signed over to the Disability Advisory Service authority to let the relevant people know, been transparent about what I needed; scheduled weekly Skype sessions with my clinical psychologist back home, and generally done everything a nerd/person with a history of this shit does to prepare for a major change.

When I got there, no-one was informed; the Skype connection in my room didn't work; and I was publicly traumatised by the head of my college at my very first event. Almost four months after the suspension of my master's, I still can't write about this without verbosity. The words vomit their way out because I was traumatised, and terrified. All of those emotions feel real. But I am also angry. And, as Natalie Portman wrote in *Harper's Bazaar*, as women, "We've been socialised to believe that we're not feeling angry – we're feeling sad, we're feeling upset (Barr, 2019)."

I am sad. I am upset. But I am also fucking irate. If you cannot provide support to students with certain conditions, do not claim that you can. It is not an easy thing to do. Ask anyone who has been the partner, friend, parent, employer of someone with a chronic mental illness. It's hard as fuck. I know that.

But to claim that you can, and then fall down so spectacularly, is to literally, actually, endanger people's lives. I almost died. More than once. That's the truth of it. Instead of helping me to make a new life for myself, Oxford almost killed me. And I don't know yet how to accept that.

P.S. If you finally find the strength to write a three-page letter outlining the various ways in which the existing systems are structurally inaccessible and destructive to someone living with mental illness and as such how your life has been placed at risk, you'll get a one-line email back saying "If you feel your life is in danger, call an ambulance."

23
Elegance in Ealing continued: Ealing, London

Midst everything else, the photoshoots continue – and I'm growing more confident with them. Every now and then, we have to reschedule because of an attack and there's a cost afterwards to putting that much energy out there – the fatigue is overwhelming as I come down. But I'm also meeting people. I find that when I'm contacting people on behalf of the shop, it's not as scary. I have a knack for making people laugh – which gets the best shots – and the easy familiarity between David and me sets them at ease. I'm also learning from the styling sessions that everyone has insecurities – no matter what they look like. I'm determined that anyone who is keen to do a photoshoot with us can. I want as wide a range of ages, races and body types as possible.

I pose another volunteer at the shop itself, using it as an opportunity to introduce our backstory to our audience – telling people how the shop opened in 2013, and was designed by two Royal College of Art students. She wears an Esprit sleeveless dress with a red bodice and navy skirt, then Ralph Lauren jeans, a Louis Feraud hot pink blazer, and black shoes from Zara. She asks if she can feature a T shirt of her own, that was designed by Daniel

Pavlovic who lives with cerebral palsy. 10% of the profits of the sale go to the Ability Centre, which supported him. Finally, she poses outside the shop in a structured red Alberta Ferretti dress.

I am getting better at pitching what we're doing, so when I approach local shop All Original, they're keen to get involved – and their staff are keen to model. The shop assistant poses for us in a baby pink Debenhams blazer over a white Topshop blouse with lace embroidery detail. She also wears statement rattan circle earrings designed by shop proprietor Jane West, and carries a unique ecofriendly handbag made from cork and sold at the shop. She poses in store wearing a floating crossover V-neckline Zara dress in yellow, with a matching fine porcelain necklace designed by Losa Lou Jewellery and sold at All Original. Finally, she wears a red Wallis dress with a fold effect under a Jane Treger black satin gown with embroidered rose sleeves – also worn with accessories sold at All Original. In the caption for this last look, I quote Phryne Fisher from the TV show *Miss Fisher's Murder Mysteries* who says that, "A woman should dress first and foremost for her own pleasure." I am so saturated with other emotions and sensations these days. But this campaign brings me pleasure.

The shop proprietor poses in a multicolour striped Missoni dress, with an orange faux leather vegan handbag from Red Cuckoo London sold in store. Jane also poses in a black lace dress from The Kooples, with a freeform wire necklace from West London designer, BijouDe Carine. Finally, she wears a floor length purple evening gown from Coast, with a lace inset and front slit.

I'm learning on each shoot – this is the first time we highlight accessories, as well as clothing from Mary's. Highlighting each look separately gives me the space to add in a snippet about the store in each caption – so that I can emphasise their focus on the handmade, local and original, and feature quotes from the jewellery designers featured.

I announce the end of our 'summer season' of photoshoots, with a write-up in the local publication *Ealing Today* entitled "Mary's Living & Giving celebrates the area with local photoshoots." In it, I write:

> Earlier this year, a new set of photographs was shared on the Instagram account @marylivingandgivingealing. They feature a woman in a sleek black evening dress with cut-outs, walking barefoot in a field of grass and trees.

The dress is a Phase Eight design, pulled from the sale rack at the Ealing branch of Mary's Living and Giving (MLG), the chain of boutique charity shops designed by retail expert Mary Portas for Save the Children in 2009. In the store, it had been donated by an Ealing resident, been sorted, steamed, tagged and priced by an Ealing volunteer and then displayed. Having not sold after a little while, it was included when a half-price sale was launched. Now, at a price of £17, it hung in the beautifully designed shop, awaiting a new owner.

When a new volunteer took over the social media for the shop, it was pulled for the first Elegance in Ealing photoshoot. Clothes are meant to be embodied. This particular dress, one of hundreds of items that move through the store with the purple front, looked so different in the photographs of volunteer model Sarah Yule in Walpole Park that shop manager Sandhya Kanabar says, "I'd put it on the sale rack only the day before, and I didn't even recognize it!"

The Elegance in Ealing photoshoots take items of clothing out of the shop, so that they can be seen in context. But not just any context. Nica Cornell, the volunteer who came up with the concept and runs the photoshoots, explains that, "As part of the community ethos of MLG, these photoshoots seek to celebrate local talent, history, sites and business. Thus far, we have done shoots at Walpole Park; The Cheddar Deli; the secondary steps of Ealing Town Hall; The Moon and Maybe; Mooch Ealing, and All Original, as well as one in our own shop. And we're just getting started!!" All the models are Ealing residents who have volunteered their time and energy, as has local filmmaker and photographer David Traub. As well as sharing the photos themselves on social media, with details on the clothing featured, each post promotes the site in question with tidbits such as The Cheddar Deli providing cheese towers for special occasions, and that Ealing Town Hall featured a public library and swimming baths when it opened in 1888.

While dependent on a limited pool of volunteer models, the photoshoots seek to show a diverse range of ethnicities, body shapes and ages. "This is particularly important to us," says Nica, "we are always working to increase the diversity of the models that we feature, as we believe that if we are going to celebrate our community, it has to be our actual community. The preparation is also such a fulfilling process – because it is for a good cause, people are willing to try things on that they wouldn't normally wear. And in the process, they are often surprised at how beautiful they look! We all have our insecurities and doubts, but it is a privilege to watch how putting on that dress that fits just right can make someone feel more confident and stand up a little taller." The MLG Instagram account has almost doubled its following in the two months since the launch of Elegance in Ealing.

Mary's Living and Giving celebrates its ten-year anniversary this year. The first boutique charity shop was launched in Edinburgh Stockbridge in 2009. There are now 26 shops across the UK, which have raised a total of £20 million for Save The Children UK. These shops are designed to be community hubs, with each being uniquely designed to reflect its neighbourhood, and run by locals. As Mary Portas says, "I wanted to create a place for people to collaborate, share, and commune, with energy, kindness and love. I wanted us to think about how we live and how we give back." Elegance in Ealing is an enactment of that ethos.

24
Breaking up on the bus: Bristol, London

A white satin shirt from a charity shop, worn under a bulky black coat, with a cream crocheted scarf crafted

> by my aunt and gifted to me back home. I wear my headphones, as I almost always do when outside of the house.

The paperwork that says we can get married arrives. They have to check it isn't some kind of stitch-up and we are actually in a relationship, which miraculously we still are.

Eight months after first being put on a list for it in Oxford, and four months after being put on a list for it in Ealing, I finally see a psychiatrist. She prescribes pregabalin, and it seems to help with the panic attacks. I'm now in the care of a mental health nurse who I don't trust, ever since she casually speculated I'm bipolar. But so long as she keeps giving me the medication lessening the panic attacks, I will keep answering her annoying calls.

On our way to Bristol, to see David's brother and his girlfriend, David's mother calls. We've already fought about his family a number of times. But momentum is carrying us along towards our October civil ceremony, until his mom phones and announces she's booked a flight to attend it (she has a British passport, as does David). We'd agreed it would be just our brothers but my brother's application for a visa has been denied. I'll have no family there, nor friends from home. But she's telling us she's coming – not asking, telling. I want to be understanding – she just wants to attend her son's wedding. But my whole body goes tense with the thought of it. I'm just keeping my skin in place as it is. My boundaries have been so unthinkably stretched by the past year that I cannot endure more changes to our plans. We arrive in Bristol already on edge. It must be obvious, although we try to pretend everything is fine. David drinks that night so I can't wake him, and I think about the fact that I have nowhere in this country to run to if I leave him.

The bus breaks down on the way back to London and I stand staring out at the countryside thinking, maybe I should just walk into the fields and run anyway? David, who knows me too well by now to try to talk, silently brings me a cup of tea from inside the roadside convenience store and walks away. It is this tenderness and consideration that breaks my train of thought and gets me back onto the back-up bus.

Once returned to London, we have to catch a train from Victoria Station, but something has gone wrong and there is almost a riot. A man shouts at the staff. A young woman is kind enough to offer me water when she sees my struggle to breathe. We escape the station onto Hyde Park where I sink down onto wet grass. I'm ravenous. David pulls out the fancy box of chocolates his brother has casually given to us. They'd received too many gifts for some event recently, this included. It burned when he did it. We don't have the money for such things. The box is pink and inspires a poem *Milkbox Tray*[1].

> *I perch in wet grass*
> *sucking chocolates I can't afford*
> *wondering if I will marry*
> *the fiancé at my side*
> *I wedge in wet dirt*
> *lifting the girl*
> *whose sight has just slipped away*
> *telling her help is coming*
> *hoping this sticky world*
> *won't make a liar out of me.*

25
Elegance in Ealing continued: Ealing, London

A bright green Zara dress with a dust ruffle hem, worn with blue suede Autograph heels.

Another photoshoot opportunity comes up at independent gift shop Mooch Ealing. No one from the store wants to pose though, and I take the leap – it doesn't feel fair to ask others to do what I won't. I agree to model.

Sandhya helps me pick the outfits for this one. There's less in my size in the store, and it's too hard to get into the usual styling mindset when the body I'm dressing is my own. I'm so used to dressing pragmatically these days, this is a novel experience. I even agree to wear blue suede Autograph heels. I'm usually still worried about the stability of my legs, but I'll only be wearing them in the shop itself, and I want to give myself fully over to this experience. Sandhya picks a sleeveless rose print Asos dress with a feature zip. I recall the first time I noticed my arms weren't as skinny as those of the popular girls at primary school. I was 11. That self-consciousness of my upper arms has never gone away, often progressing to outright loathing. To be photographed against the store's signage wearing something sleeveless, when my arms are bigger than they've ever been – as am I – feels liberating. Inside, I pose in a leopard print camel coloured Gina Bacconi dress. I'm seated so my tummy rolls are obvious. Again, I am somewhat liberated by this. This is my new body, and it's mine to dress and show. Finally, I wear a bright green Zara dress with a dust ruffle hem – and something happens that's happening more and more when I do these shoots. The model buys the dress! I usually can't afford things at the shop, which specialises in designer clothing. But this dress is £10, and I decide I deserve a reward for my hard work and progress. I run into a local artist at Ealing BEAT, the local art trail, I'm also photographing for the Instagram, and she tells me she remembers donating the dress.

We follow this shoot up with our first man's photoshoot – he's the son of a volunteer, and he poses happily with his dog in Walpole Park. Ealing Toy Library contacts me via Instagram to ask if we can do a photoshoot with their founders, two local mums that want to reduce wastage. In our posts, I highlight that 90% of toys are made of plastic, have lower lifespans than other plastic items, and are particularly challenging to recycle. I quote the Greenpeace Science Unit who told Huffington Post in 2017 that, "As soon as you open it, you'll be putting it in the waste stream." We have particular fun doing their photoshoot, because their three young kids are running around our legs at the time. I am so besotted with them that I basically leave the shoot to David, and spend most of the time pulling funny faces.

We follow this up by featuring a local silversmith who, under the moniker of Ange B Designs, creates sculptural jewellery in her designated She Cave shed in her back garden in Ealing. David's favourite part of this shoot, wherein we use simple block colours of clothing from the shop to provide contrast to the jewellery Ange is wearing, is filming her at work with her tools. I like how the cutout in the back of the aquamarine Jaeger dress allows the perfect space for the long backdrop of her Bib necklace to hang on her skin. We are about to order my wedding ring off Etsy from a Cornish silversmith, as I have Cornish familial roots and am desperate for some sense of my family on the day. The ring I've chosen is engraved with the shape of waves of the ocean – and is entitled the 'Rough Seas' ring which feels apt. Ange does us the favour of measuring my fingers, which are larger than they used to be (the only part of my body unchanged is my feet), and telling us my ring size.

I reach out to the local Business Improvement District to discuss featuring our campaign in their newsletter. Somewhat intimidatingly, I get an email saying the Chief Executive Officer herself will come down to meet me at the shop to discuss it. I sit in the basement room of Mary's, where all the clothes are stored, sorted and steamed before they go upstairs to the shop floor. I'm wearing a loose, sleeveless top with a space print that belonged to my mom in the 1980s. I can feel myself shrivelling slightly when Gerry arrives in her sharp suit, with her sleek blonde haircut. I'm suddenly acutely aware of my arms, which I'm shy of even on a good day. I'm certain she's going to think, "What could she possibly know about fashion?" But once we get chatting, Gerry is happy to feature our campaign – she's clearly passionate about her work promoting Ealing Town Centre as a "great place to work, live and play." She even seems impressed with me – asking about my background, and telling me that they're going to be advertising a new role soon that she thinks will suit me.

26
Pregnancy scare: Ealing, London

My navy close-fitted matric jersey (they call it a jumper here), with white and red piping.

My condition is currently classified as moderate major depressive disorder, with a panic disorder (added for seasoning and spice). As David says, how are you meant to not be depressed after a year of near-constant panic? Not just worries, or stress, or any of the other everyday experiences that anyone living in a world that is eating itself would have. As my friend and I agreed recently, it's the people who are calm in 2019 that terrify us – did anyone else read the outgoing interview of the fired/resigned/who-really-knows-with-Trump national security advisor who says the reason there haven't been any more nuclear missile tests by North Korea is they're pretty confident they've got that shit sorted? The calm people are terrifying.

But this is different. This is chemical, adrenaline-pumping, hands-trembling, upper-lip sweating, panic. For 365 days. In a row. No wonder I'm bloody tired. It's fairly miraculous I can make a cup of tea at this point. They've medicated the physical symptoms down or away, one pill at a time. But the actual panic? Not so much. Still, there's a new pill this week – two in fact, so here's hoping. Two of the same one, because the psychiatrist I finally got to see seems to know what she is doing and doesn't whack you on diazepam three times a day for months and then express confusion when you can't, you know, walk or talk.

I was 16 when I was first diagnosed. I remember it vividly. I remember walking to meet my mom at a café afterwards with relief and even something akin to hope. I wasn't just deficient. Something was wrong, and it wasn't me.

That was a decade ago now. When I met with the reasonable psychiatrist, I couldn't remember the names of all the medications I've been put on and taken off. I had to write off to a doctor's surgery in a town whose name has been changed to find out what the chap there put me on for a year five years ago.

I can't answer all those medical questions nowadays, and it gets in the way sometimes.

How to explain?

I remember all the things it's taken. I remember falling face first onto my brother after kissing him goodnight because I'd been given Valium. I remember not being able to feel anything the first times I had sex because paroxetine causes sexual dysfunction. I remember crawling up the steps of my department at Oxford because diazepam had taken my legs. I remember knowing I was going to sink in the pool mid-stroke because venaflaxine is different to desvenaflaxine. I remember the humiliation of falling, shaking, on my knees in my first master's class. I remember having a hot flush on a train and thinking I was going to suffocate. I remember being hungry because I was unable to cook dinner because I couldn't stand long enough; or order food, because my college building had stairs and I couldn't make it down them. I remember wandering Oxford in a panic disorder and diazepam-induced haze, and almost being hit by a truck. I remember lying face down, naked, where I had fallen on the dry blue carpet of my residence room and not being able to get up.

I remember my mother saying depression is a rational response to an irrational world.

I remember my father saying I have depression because I don't exercise enough.

I remember it being an achievement that I walked in the park alone.

Today is my first solo appointment with my mental health nurse, meaning not only that I go in alone, but that I actually get myself there alone. I pass the Marie Stopes clinic and the cluster of camped out anti-abortion protesters who are always sitting in camper chairs on the opposite corner; check myself in on the little digital screen; and sit in the waiting room alone; managing the rising panic all along the way, taking off my English-winter-has-begun jersey even though I couldn't find a bra, for the sweat.

And then, midway through a reasonably manageable appointment, I tell her I've been vomiting a bit. I make clear I'm dealing with a pretty large number of stressful things, even apart from having a debilitating mental illness. I'm getting married in a foreign country on Monday, so there's that. I won't have any family there, except in the tiny ribbon I will wrap around my South African protea flowers if I can find them, cut from my first ever dress and currently being sewn into a ribbon by the local Ghanaian tailor then brought across the seas from my mom by my about-to-be mother-in-law who is arriving the night before the wedding. There's that, and a whole lot of other stuff, which I shared with the nurse. They also just changed my dosage of the medication they had also just changed. So…my body understands that it isn't on a beach holiday in Pringle Bay.

So, I say, "I've been vomiting." "Any chance of pregnancy?" She asked without looking up from her screen with its disingenuously tidy list of side effects. "No, I just had my period." "Well, some women keep having them. You should take a test just so we know." Casual like that. "And then you'll need to fill out this form for the new prescription, and it may take two days (sorry about your wedding). Also remember we're all sad sometimes, and listen to music that makes you happy. Have you had any thoughts of harming yourself?" "No." "Any thoughts of harming anyone else?" Not until about five seconds ago…

Now, caution is good, I'm totally there for the people who are in charge of which psychiatric drugs I take being cautious. But you also can't just drop that shit on me. Two days before my wedding. In a foreign country. Without family or friends.

So, that's what I get to do the Friday before I get married. I get to go to the pharmacy alone to buy the cheapest pregnancy test the chap behind the counter can scratch up. Not because my fiancé isn't supportive. He is supportive – he's bloody working until 8 pm.

She knew it was my first appointment alone. She knew all the things she could possibly know without me literally cutting my head open for her to dig around in.

But also, you might be pregnant and that's the kind of thing we like to know, so why not pop off to get a test?

I'm not pregnant. I am pissed.

27
Trousseau: Ealing, London

Ornate labradorite and mother of pearl earrings, bought from a little jewelery stall in the Red Shed at the Victoria

and Albert Waterfront (yes, it's still called that over 50 years after the end of British rule) in Cape Town, South Africa.

I've been a doctor's receptionist before – for the woman about to become my mother-in-law, if I can go through with the civil ceremony that is a day away. I've been throwing up for the nerves – every night, like clockwork. For all I am feeling smothered by her now, she is an astonishing doctor. A proper GP who knows your context, not just your symptoms. I should know. She'd been my doctor too, long before I'd known her son. Even he'd been a receptionist for her – that's my first memory of him as a man, not a boy. Noticing him behind the counter, alert to his handsome features at that age where any such encounter stirs up a story of possibility in one. We'd both been skilled at it – being polite to people in distress, greeting everyone with a wide smile. I liked the sense of purpose and that I was helping people to get what they needed. I didn't like the men who looked down my blouse or the slimy pharmaceutical reps. Well, no matter. They've replaced us with a touchscreen pad. We're now the couple in distress – a story come true, years in the making. Her engagement ring is loose. The arc of his body protective, hunched around her, tuned in to her body's silent cues – he knows there's an attack coming before she does these days. He has become her hypervigilance. Such is their young love.

I buy wedding accessories with fastidious attention. The shoes are secondhand Steve Madden teal platform heels on which Sandhya gave me a discount. I buy a white birdcage veil on Etsy (where I spend a lot of time in the night when David is sleeping and I cannot), unwrapped on a bench in Walpole Park at the Rickyard café where we like to meet for coffee during his lunch breaks. The delicate white flowers evoke the silk flowers my great aunt used to paint. The veil is a testament to another elegant aunt's black one that lay on her hat hook outside her guest bedroom. It was almost funereal, but I coveted it.

I buy a teal velvet hair scrunchie, to keep my hair off my neck, from ASOS Marketplace. My wedding earrings are my own kind of heirloom. They're a decade old – bought with vouchers for the colonially monikered Victoria & Albert Waterfront in Cape Town, given out by my first high school for academic awards. I'd stocked up a wallet full mid-way through high school and I wanted to buy something special. A diamond was really what I wanted, without any sense of their cost – I am the prospector Frederick Carruthers Cornell's great-granddaughter, after all. But all the shops took one look at my 13-year-old cousin and me, even in our best teenage outfits, and sniffed their way past us. These were the shops we walked past on our way to the movies, not ones we normally looked at, never mind went in. Their shine was for tourists or Cape Town's elite, which – despite being white in South Africa – we certainly were not. It was making for a horrid disappointment of a Saturday, until we stumbled on a little jewellery store called Juliana's in the Red Shed which usually specialised in crafts. Here there were beautiful jewels – and a kind woman who welcomed us into the store. She told us we could try on anything we liked – she'd clean the earrings for us with spirits if we opted for those. I'd never have even tried on these earrings had she not encouraged me. But I was enchanted by their elaborate labradorite weavings, and moonstone drops. I felt a queen the moment they were on, none of that princess malarkey for me. I'd always been fixated on royalty anyway – and

I was still in the throes of my British royal family indoctrination. My mom always said I got it from my gran. I definitely didn't get it from anyone else in my massive subversive family. The earrings hung long and pristine. They were beyond my voucher budget. But I was earning money as a writer, at that young age already, even if I tended not to spend it. I could technically afford them. I said that day on the way home after my mom picked us up, I'd wear them to get married.

I just never imagined a meeting room with a registrar, not a cousin nor my mother in sight. I am so desperate for a familial connection that I order a ring made by a Cornish silversmith. It costs £27, which seems a fortune to me. My great-grandmother was Cornish. I am desperate to find a story that makes sense of this, some kind of 'return' narrative when all I feel is thoroughly lost. I am marrying the man I love to stay in this country with him. But I'm not sure I like this country at all and from what I can tell, the feeling is mutual.

On the day, my about-to-be brother-in-law will hand the ring to me from a carved box I bought from the artist who made it – the shape of Africa with Kenya as its key (in case you couldn't tell from which country he came) at a market in a tiny, terrible town back home. His smile was genuine, and I leaned into it with relief, escaping the horror of my surroundings. I've loved that box, and it has travelled with me, a piece of home, an emblem of my continent. And each time I feel the slide of the stone and it reveals its secrets, I am 16, alone at a market, and my heart is easing.

My about to be mother-in-law offers to pay for a manicure and pedicure, some kind of pampering. It is a kind gesture. But I can't take her up on it. It is too much – strangers touching me, moving around in my peripheral vision, talking to me. Going into an unfamiliar space. I opt for bare nails for this ceremony. It is a ceremony. There will be words. They send us a few possible scripts, and we choose one. I like it well enough. It's simple and about the circle of love which is a visual that comforts me. There'll be no reference to a God of any kind. I'm not religious but I'm deeply spiritual. Nonetheless, this is a legal process. My about to be mother-in-law takes us to dinner the night before. She talks to us about how we keep putting up walls when we need to lean into them. I can't bear it. I don't even know why. I am barely a person, more leaking sensation and these entreaties scrape on my flayed boundaries. I have nothing here that is mine, except a few belongings and my aching self. I am protecting myself as desperately as I can. She offers to buy me a bouquet in the morning. I won't be able to make my own choice that way. I will feel obliged to do something that satisfies someone else. I am unequivocal, rigid, brittle with pain – this ceremony must be on my terms in some tiny way, or I'm going to shatter with the terror of what I'm doing and feeling.

I go home that night. David's mother's words have gone over his head while they stick like peanut butter in mine. I submit my job application for the Business Improvement District, Make It Ealing. They are looking for someone to do their communications and I'd clicked with the CEO when we met. David edits my CV which is a tangle of the freelance gigs I worked to get here. Transcription, writing, editing, tutoring, retail. A year's work went into the application, flight and visa fees until I was awarded a scholarship to Oxford. Now there is a half degree on the document that will decide whether I'm ever self-sufficient again. David is supporting us, with help from his parents. He does it without complaint. I've been earning for myself since I was 14 and got a column in a national newspaper. This is a painful experience, having no money of my own. I've gotten to know the area's businesses, as we've done various photoshoots in them. By now, I've featured 42 different outfits from Mary's on our Instagram at eight different locations. I've gotten a sense of what it means to be a part of this community and to contribute to it. I know nothing about business, but I have an intuitive grasp of communications and once I understand business to be about people's livelihoods it makes sense to me – even if the jargon is abruptly new. David tells me my CV is formatted poorly for this new country. I let him fix it before I send it in. I've not much confidence in my own instincts anymore – how can I when he knows my bodily cues better than I do?

28
Morning of marriage: Ealing, London

Black bicycle shorts worn underneath jeans from a Cats Protection charity shop in Northfields, London.

It's 6 AM and my eyes are wide. I can count on my fingers how many times I've left the flat alone in the past months. But the day of our civil ceremony has come, and the reality is making my skin itch. David opens his eyes to the sight of me pulling jeans on over shorts, in my hurry to get out. He must think I am running, something I have thought about more than once as the enormity of it all overwhelms me. If I'd had somewhere to run that didn't involve getting on a plane, I may well have backed out. I love him. There's no goddamn question of that. He's doing his best to manage what is a wildly unmanageable situation every day. It's just too much for my soul to handle some days. Most of them, really. He has been utterly calm since the day he came home from the pub and finally named what we were doing anyway: Let's just get married. I have not. I am terrified. I'm too young, too ill, too foreign, too poor … too everything … to be a wife, his wife. But today I will be, nonetheless. It occurs to me once I stand on the dirty, crumbling steps to our building, that flowers picked in Walpole Park would be the most appropriate for a bouquet. It has held us, through my learning to walk again, through photoshoots for Elegance in Ealing, through coffee dates when we were going nowhere else. We've watched the mallards, tufted ducks, herons, moorhens, and Canadian geese, make their families through the spring that is now ended – and learned their species names for the very first time. I've learned every path and it has just about kept me sane, with its tall trees, yellow and orange flowers, and parakeets. The story goes that they were brought in for Ealing Studios when they filmed *Out of Africa*, to 'indigenise' the set (never mind where parakeets are actually from) and some got out. They've been adding their lime green and burnt orange colour palettes to Ealing's streets ever since. I was lying beneath my favourite tree once and looked up into a pair of them gently nuzzling.

A not-wedding bouquet from there would be apt. The symbols matter to me dearly. My about to be mother-in-law has brought totems of home across the seas from South Africa, smelling of my own mother. These include a video that my family have put together wishing us the best, which I watched teary eyed the night before; a postcard from my aunt of the old post office in Tintagel, where my great-grandmother was from, in Cornwall before she married my great-grandfather and they travelled to South Africa; another aunt's gifts are a vintage bridal nightgown in peach satin and white lace panties that are both too taut for this new post-panic body; and a ribbon for my bouquet my mother has had made from the hem of my very first dress, which ironically was made up in broderie anglaise. I'm planning to drape that white ribbon around my bouquet of hand-picked flowers from the park we cherish.

It's a glistening winter morning so I find the park is frozen over, without a fresh flower in sight. I make a slapdash decision to do something I never do alone and go to the shopping centre, Ealing Broadway. My shorts are chafing as I take slightly too long strides and listen to my big cousin's iteration of Happy Birthday, made into a Happy Wedding Day song, on WhatsApp. I make it to Tesco as it is opening. There is no-one there but the staff, and I wonder what the security guard makes of the wildness in my movements. I have strayed 5 minutes outside of the radius I have cautiously carved, now desperate to get flowers for a bouquet after having turned down my mother-in-law's offer the previous night. I'm here so early they only have the day-old flowers out. I find a marked down bouquet. I can't name the flowers, some of which are drooping. But there is a single stern-stemmed white flower and a two-headed burgundy flower. They remind me somehow of the time one of my South African therapists, Sorayah, ran after me to give me a flower after my appointment – a two-headed yellow rose that she said resembled me: "beautiful and unusual". I've almost no money in my account these days, especially post pregnancy kit, but I can afford this as my not-wedding bouquet. I make it back home with my prize, gleaming with sweat but somehow proud. I've done this one thing for myself.

I dress alone too. There are no bridesmaids flitting about nor proud parents in the corner, trying to stay out of the way of the hair and make-up teams. It's me who ties my hair back off my neck; slides the birdcage veil into place; pens a line of black eyeliner on my lower lid & carefully shapes my lips in red.

My about-to-be husband takes a video of my preparations, knowing I have always wanted shots of my getting ready on my wedding day. I'm that girl. I've been plotting this day since before my dad left when I was 9. This is not what I imagined but we make do. David has bought nothing new. He wears a pair of suit pants from Primark, the crotch of which he glued back together for his grandfather's funeral, and a purple shirt. I realise at the last moment it's fucking British winter. I'll need a coat over my floating chiffon duck-blue #177407 Evening Gown from JJ's House. I'm using its forgiving silhouette to cover the massive changes my body has undergone since I stopped being able to stand for very long. I pull a black velvet opera coat from the white wooden cupboard that we'd bought from British Heart Foundation. I've never worn it, having bought it when David gifted me £50 to shop for clothes at the specialised vintage store in Oxford on my birthday. I'd drooled over its contents and then decided to opt for the charity shop where I'd bought them out of everything I wanted. This coat was part of that haul. I am wearing high platform heels in velvet teal, holding up the long flow of my dress, as I make my way down our front steps. I always think neighbours must think David is particularly chivalrous. He is – but that's not why he helps me down these stairs every time. It's still a question of whether my legs will tremble or fall. Sandhya has agreed to serve as my witness at the wedding. She and her husband arrive shortly, chic as ever, my surrogate parents for the day. I'm meeting her husband for the first time this day. They've pronounced, with the generosity of found family, that they'll drive me – and paid for us to have a night in the Richmond Hotel, as someone had done the same for them when they'd married. Sandhya says simply pass it on someday when someone needs it. Otherwise, we were simply heading back to the flat. David only has the day of the ceremony and the day after off – then it's back to work and I return to the labour of recovery. Dipak and Sandhya drive us to Haringey, and it is a long drive for me. I've got barn owls in my belly. We talk about weddings, and I talk about how you don't need a big, frivolous affair. It's expensive and unnecessary. I'm fooling no one with my insistence.

29
Civil ceremony: Haringey, London

A floating chiffon duck blue evening gown.

We arrive and are early for our morning ceremony, as I always am thanks to my mom's punctuality. There are other couples waiting. Someone suggests a coffee so I find myself in a greasy spoon in an evening gown. David's dad calls to speak to him. We head across the busy road, me tottering in my heels, but we're still too early. I don't want to take photos before. I've already said that. I say I'm going outside for some air, too tense to sit in this hallway with strangers. They're all strangers in some ways. David's mom follows, telling everyone to come outside for some photographs. I look to David but he says nothing. Now I am posing for photographs with people who will shortly be my family. I am discomfited and say I'm going inside to the bathroom. I need a moment to myself, to reckon with the vastness of what's happening, to buck up my courage. David's mom says she'll join me. I don't want to be rude but I also want to scream. David says nothing. This is not boding well, but we've already had our fight about her coming and I am now in the not-wedding dress, for fuck's sake. She was wounded he didn't welcome her surprise announcement. He was frustrated she didn't ask him before buying a ticket but also does want her there. Mostly however he was tense with the knowledge that I was holding on by a degraded string. I need my boundaries to matter, even when they are absurd – I have so little choice in anything that's happening to me, subject to the brute force of immigration law and my body's breakdown. In the bathroom, she tells me my hair looks so pretty down as I redo it. I tell her I want it up. My mother is not here, and it is agony.

I make my slow way down the staircase, trying to stabilise my breath. I'm not wearing blusher, just flushed with heat. Finally, we are at the front of the queue. The registrar's assistant, a kindly middle-aged black woman with a large white birthmark on her face, calls us in to confirm some details on the form, and then asks if I want to walk down the aisle. It's so unexpected for something so… normal … to crop up in a process that feels saturated with strange. It has not even occurred to me that I will walk down an aisle today. She smiles at me – and offers again, saying they have music they can play as we haven't brought any. So, I wait outside until she calls me in, everyone else having gone ahead, alone in the corridor where I am sick with nerves. Finally, she comes to say the music is about to begin and I can enter when it does. I walk into the medium-sized taupe room and make my way between the two banks of chairs. David, for the first time in this entire process, looks like he is melting. And seeing him, then standing up there with him, I am suddenly overcome with giddiness. How funny it all is. The registrar is a thin white man with his own wide smile. He feels like my principal at my last high school – smiling with genuine pleasure as I receive awards. His British twang makes David's surname sound funny. Everything suddenly sounds funny to me. David's brother worrying at the

Civil ceremony: Haringey, London

chain of the necklace David's opted for instead of a ring, trying to disentangle it in time for the exchange. David's mom is recording us. I don't even mind that I wasn't asked. He's holding my hand and we're here, by some miracle. I remember that I wanted this long before Oxford broke me, or the Home Office threatened me. The registrar stumbles over the word necklace – saying ring and his assistant corrects him as a schoolmarm. I'm finding it genuinely difficult not to break out into peals of laughter. Why is everyone so serious? I feel my right earring sliding out of my ear – as it slips onto my shoulder, I palm it quickly into David's hand. No one else even notices it, this tiny moment of symbiosis, we're paying such acute attention to each other. He is handsome, and he is becoming my husband – even England is going to have to recognise that. In your face, England. He knows me, and he still loves me.

There's been nothing light about this love for a while now – it's held up as we've registered him as my carer at the doctor's. He is 25, a year younger than I. It's held up as he's come home from a full day's work and had to cook because I can't stand that long. It's held up as I've volunteered him to volunteer alongside me for the charity shop. It's held up as he's spent evening after evening at the pub with his friends as I've been unable to manage the noise or triggers enough to join them. It's held up but we've both been carrying the weight of these experiences, a ship that's taken on too much water and is a long way from shore.

Here we are now, and I remember I'm staying for a reason. Here we are now, and I remember what it's like to float.

30
Reception: Richmond, London

A cobalt Bardot neckline Lindy Bop midi dress, with space for a petticoat beneath its wide skirt.

We're at the Nepalese restaurant that we found once on a spur-of-the-moment Google. The food here, at Monty's in Ealing, is superb, so we've phoned and made a booking. They've put up gold balloons and given us a private room because we told them it's a wedding – although once again I've been standing on the pavement in my almost-bridal wear, waiting for the restaurant to open. The world has certainly not stopped for us – despite my being a wife, when I wasn't this morning. The world is going ostentatiously on. We've arranged a meal, and I've organised a 'cake' from the Cheddar Deli. A small cheese tower. I've had to drag David's opinion out of him, to decide what will adorn this tower, but eventually he was oddly specific. He wants a doll's house–sized wedding cake on top, along with a miniature version of our calico cat. It has taken a significant number of hours on the internet to find the two, but I've done it. I'm pleased with the outcome – it's quirky and unusual, but it represents the things that are good about the life we've made. Our regular trips to the Cheddar Deli as a treat, this miniature almost-wedding, and the home we've made for our cat. I'm attached to this and put out when it is overshadowed by the two-tier wedding cake my new mother-in-law surprises us with. She has brought it from Bristol and so desperately wants us to be pleased, so I try, but am conflicted. Once again, the way I have wanted things on this strange occasion where so much is beyond my control is somehow not enough. The cake is caramel and banana, two flavours I dislike.

We decide to Uber to the hotel, so overwhelmed by even this small group of people by this point. Neither of us really knows how to feel. David's mother is kindly spending the night at our flat, taking care of the Bean. We've never left her for a night before. We arrive at the hotel, where there's a mix-up with the payment. We spend time sorting it out at the desk, my long black velvet coat covering my dress. We finally make our way to the room. It's cosy and they've put out a plate saying congratulations in chocolate with strawberries. I eat the strawberries and we fall fast asleep for hours, finally relaxed. It's done. We've done it. We both made it through this precious and peculiar day.

We wake up and I change into a cobalt midi dress from Lindy Bop, with a Bardot neckline and space for a petticoat beneath the skirt, bought from a lovely charity shop on Bond Street. We make our way down to the lavish and gleaming restaurant. We eat, and I tell David how I felt about my wishes not being respected as we waited for the ceremony. It's gone entirely over his head. I know I am a raw nerve to every perceived slight. But how could I not be? I am brimming with feelings that all clash up against each other, an artist's palette of inks *ingemengde* (mixed together in Afrikaans). They're sitting above the neckline of my dress before they flow straight out of my mouth. I tell a stranger in the bathroom that we got married today because I feel someone should know. I return to my table, and she comes to tap on my shoulder – her and her partner are seated by the fire, in the prime spot of the hotel. She's offering us their seat because we're newlyweds. I am deeply touched by this stranger's act of kindness, able to receive it in its wholeness without feeling threat or expectation. We sit at the fire and order an after-dinner drink. The fire reflects in the basin of the glasses, as we try to absorb the enormity of the day.

31
Wife: Ealing, London

A black velvet opera coat, from an Oxford charity shop.

It's the next day and we are strolling through the crisp air on Richmond Hill. The woman in the café, upon hearing we're newlyweds, gives us a chocolate brownie – she tells me that in her country, it is tradition to give newlyweds something sweet. Again, I am touched by this reaching out in this foreign land. We stumble across the Angelina Colarusso store, and I am entranced by the dress in the window. It is my dream wedding dress. It is a moment that feels portentous, offering me a promise for the future. We've already agreed we will have a big grand wedding back in South Africa as soon as we can. That's how I've held the line through the past 24 hours – knowing I've compromised on this day I've, foolishly or not, been fixated on all my life. Knowing that the day will come, and ultimately knowing David is the right groom, whatever else I've given up. He shows it to me all the time. We sit on the bus on the way home, arriving to our usually messy flat fully cleaned (including the inside of the oven) by David's mom. I cannot help but feel embarrassed. It has taken everything we had to get to the civil ceremony. There's been no energy to spare for cleaning. I hide my face in the bedroom, going straight to bed.

David is back at work. It's the day after the day after, and I am once again alone in the flat. Something irrevocable has been altered by the saying of a few words, but much remains the same. I lean into stereotype and cook a meal for David to welcome him home from work. We eat together, saying grace to Someone. I was raised by a lapsed Catholic, with a deep sense of spirituality. He is Jewish. Neither of us really cares who we are praying to these days. Anyone who will answer.

32
Immigrant: Croydon, London

Black suede boots, black jeans and a black blouse.

We've begun to prepare the visa application, now that we're married. I have a panic attack at the train station en route to our first appointment with the fancy lawyer we've paid from David's inheritance (claimed ahead of time). We meet her online. She seems nice. I am comforted that she has African roots herself. She tells me I don't have to do the English test, and I am relieved, mainly because I find them offensive. English is spoken in South Africa as a result of British colonisation. We pay an accountant money we can barely afford to write a letter we are then told we do not need. David begins working full-time at the film school where he's been working part-time. This makes him a fit financial sponsor for the visa. We take two trains across London to the biometrics appointment. It takes me an attack and a half to get there. We find the lawyer has not told us what paperwork to take so we're not allowed into the building. We cough up for an Uber home, and I am caved in. We reach the safety of Ealing's lights but I do not think I can take any more, never mind do this trip again.

I get an email – I've got a job interview for the Business Improvement District. I've posted every day for Mary's Living and

Giving for over six months. It gives me joy, reaching out from my little safe flat even when I can't leave it, celebrating the community highlights we've discovered, making the wide range of models feel as beautiful as they are. I go for the interview in black jeans, boots and a blouse, hoping this trifecta of B's is formal enough as it's the most formal I've got. The building where they're holding the interviews is grand and intimidating. David drops me off out front with perceptive advice – on the two questions I'm most nervous about. My immigration status and my health. I am better than I was, but neither is stable. He says, "Tell the truth. That's all you can do. If they choose to hire you, they have to know anyway." Brilliant advice but easier said than done. I am called into the room to face the three of them. I explain about my immigration situation – that we've just married and are about to put in a spousal application. Our lawyer assures us the visa will happen within a matter of weeks.

I refer in an early answer to my education. They ask what I'm referring to. Instead of reformatting my degree, it turns out that David has accidentally removed the one thing I've got going for me. I have two and a half degrees. I got into Oxford on full scholarship – even if it turned out to be a monstrous experience. I make a joke about killing my husband (the word still feels naïve in my mouth) and explain that we sent the application in the night before the civil ceremony. I quickly run through my qualifications. They seem to care less about the suspending of my degree at Oxford than that I got in. I can see it's impressed them. Well, at least something has. I feel less impressive by the second. I answer frankly about my health, explaining that it is unpredictable. I emphasise that my recovery is tied to my relationship with this place – that I can't make sense of living in England, with its soaked weather and aggressive immigration policies, but I have come to love Ealing. My sense of the local has been central to our successful campaign Elegance in Ealing, and it has been a journey of discovery as I've come into it with new eyes. There's been an urgency to my getting to know it that they will struggle to find in someone else.

I leave the interview, and sob for hours. I'm so embarrassed. How could I send them a CV missing a page. I am unprofessional. My messiness is showing, even to strangers – grey suited businesspeople who have titles after their names and know things. I know I've not got the job. David says I should be proud I went for it. That kind of pride in myself is far beyond me.

I get a phone call from the CEO. They have more questions about my immigration situation. I answer honestly with the knowledge I have. Mostly, I'm in shock. They want me. Someone here, in England, wants to give me a job with Business in the title *nogal* (on top of everything else in Afrikaans).

We go for our next biometrics appointment. The room is full of tense families, with numerous children. No one here is happy. Everyone is afraid. It's an outsourced company. The staff are nice enough. It's not their fault they are the face of the Home Office for us. The Home Office who decide whether your life is enough or you have 28 days to leave the country.

The room is heaving. The system was down the day before and everyone who had appointments was told to return today. The tension is bubbling over. A man is shouting. Everyone's fear is loud and the crowd outside is beginning to lose control.

33
New job: Ealing, London

A loose black blazer from Zara, worn over a loose navy-blue dress from Coast.

I am all wrong for this. I underdress on my first day at the office – Gerry points out that I should not wear jeans and *takkies* (running shoes) going forwards. I overdress on my second day on the job – a now too tight black pencil skirt left over from my *sub fusc* days at Oxford, black stockings and heeled black boots, and a red coat for the weather because I know we're at our stand at the Christmas market in Ealing Broadway all day. I feel clumsy and out of practice at having anything much to dress for – my shoes are all wrong for a day when I'm on my feet, and my skirt too tight for kneeling down to help the kids make Christmas baubles. But I do it anyway. Elegance in Ealing has taught me I'm skilled at setting people at ease. I play with the children, happily, and chat to their parents about our local community. After all my hard work getting to know it and celebrating it, it feels like something I share in now. I make a bauble for our own Christmas tree, bought at the local Pines and Needles in the grounds of the church where I like to say my prayers. David carries it home on his shoulder and we film it popping out of its netting.

Hearing I don't have the right clothes for work, and knowing we can't afford to buy some, Sandhya – as a thank you for all my volunteering - opens the shop early on a Saturday and kits me out with a few outfits from the shop, including a loose black Zara blazer, fitted black cigarette trousers, and a navy-blue dress from Coast.

34
Newlywed: Ealing, London

Boat neck black velvet dress, gifted to me by Sandhya as a thank you for all my hard work with Elegance in Ealing. I wear it with black sheer stockings, black shorts I wear under all dresses and skirts so my thighs do not chafe, and black heeled suede boots.

We go for a pub dinner on Christmas Eve at The Drapers Arms pub. The food is superb. I don't usually go out after dark, which circumscribes life a lot in winter here where the sun sets early. It's a treat. David's working and I've just gotten a job. Our visa application is in. The pub is vast, an old factory site, and seasonally decorated with holly on the tables in small bottles. We bask in the gold of candlelight, seated in two deep armchairs with a view of the giant lit-up Christmas bauble on the grass outside. It's a Christmas installation by my new employer.

Aged 9, I 'married' my Grade 3 boyfriend in a black velvet gown – a copy of my aunt's wedding gown, made for her daughter to wear as bridesmaid at her parents' wedding. Black velvet has always been luxurious and chic to me, embodying the glamour of my mom's big sister with her brunette hair piled up on her head and tower of Ferrero Rocher wedding cake. The Drapers

Arms pub is at the end of our street – a five-minute walk from home – so I am wearing heels. I have come to trust that my legs will work, for the most part. It is not as it was in this very same pub months before, when I arrived on trembling legs, drenched with sweat and lugging a blue suitcase.

At first glance, we are just a young couple in London celebrating our first Christmas as newlyweds. For once, no panic slips out from under my dress, to reveal the horrors of the past year. I'm wearing the 'touch of colour' on my lips that my granny always recommended. I am briefly whole.

35
Elegance in Ealing continued: Ealing, London

A Joe Browns textured dress with matching grey boots.

We share our only couple's photoshoot with Houseful of Clocks in the days ahead of New Year 2019. On Boxing Day a few years earlier, Sharon had fallen in love with an old Smiths electric clock at an antiques bazaar. She asked her husband Martin, who'd previously restored vintage motorbikes and furniture, to fix it. Soon they were running out of space for all the clocks Martin restored and she suggested they start selling them. To suit the art deco vibe of the vintage clocks which we feature prominently in the photos, in one series of photos, Martin dresses in Burton Menswear pinstripe trousers with a felt cap, and Sharon wears a BDL black gown with a scooped back and satin stripe. In another, Martin wears a Reiss suit with a Bloomingdale's 100% silk tie and Sharon wears a Pretty Little Thing gold lame dress with Cloves champagne gloves – a rare cream and black Bakelite Smiths clock posed between them. Finally, Martin wears a Reiss suit with a geometric print Van Heusen tie and Sharon models a Coast olive halter neck dress with a vintage faux fur jacket from Mary's.

Elegance in Ealing is shortlisted for a Digital Impact Award by the Modern Retail Good Retail Awards which celebrate retailers that are making a positive impact and our campaign reaches its pinnacle with a special cover photoshoot for Ealing Council's *Around Ealing* magazine, on the importance of sustainable fashion. It features a local mum, social media manager, and charity organiser – and a fellow South African – wearing a green polo-neck Scotch & Soda dress styled with leopard print Migato heeled boots and a layered Coreen necklace, posing at Gunnersbury Park.

Less than a year after moving to Ealing, my concept is being delivered to every home in the borough.

On International Women's Day, we share the final series of photos from that photoshoot, with Yolanda wearing a Jus d'Orange Paris purple cowl-neck dress, with a message directly from David and me: "The heart of this project has been the 1:1 styling sessions at Mary's Living and Giving Ealing. The trust, honour & courage shown by our models in this intimate setting is what we have sought to show in our photographs. It's been an honour to work with such a range of dynamic & glorious women. We hope we've done you proud."

36
Calamity: Ealing, London

A black Zara blazer, worn with unbranded black cigarette trousers bought from a charity shop.

We wait for news on the visa. And we wait – making half-plans for what to do if it's a no. I look into how you transport a cat overseas, and wonder if the Bean will survive the trip.

At work, I'm working my way up, one day a week, then two, then three – checking in on my health as I go. For the most part, I've settled in well, run a Christmas raffle, and a successful social media campaign around the giant lit-up teddy bear we've installed for Valentine's Day on the patch of grass on Ealing Green. I've ordered a regular-sized teddy bear, and dressed it in a red jumper to match. I've taken it to visit our various businesses and we've taken fun pictures of it posing having a haircut at Yuzu's salon, pouring a pint at Draper's Arms and shopping for fresh groceries at Reineta. We've used the photos on our social media to promote our businesses and the Valentine's Day teddy bear installation.

When no word on my visa comes for months, and it was meant to take weeks, we lodge an enquiry with the Home Office. I get a brief phone call back at work – the Home Office sent the response to our lawyer months ago.

My boss takes one look at my face and says I can go home. I am on the phone with David, passing the Starbucks in Ealing Broadway, frantically trying to explain what was said. It takes him an age to chase down our lawyer, whom we paid an extortionate amount. Finally, she answers the phone and tracks down our paperwork that she says she was too busy to notify us about. Our application has been rejected. It's difficult to concentrate on the reasons, the distress is so physical and immediate.

Ultimately, she admits she gave us poor advice on how to substantiate our finances and did not tell us I needed to submit a test proving I speak English (the one I did when I first came here no longer counts, nor do the two degrees I got from an English medium university). She has filed an appeal, and the big immigration law firm she works for will be covering the cost of it as they know it was their error. The appeal will take years to get to court. It's already been a year since I was home, and I've almost died, and married, in that year. During the wait, I cannot leave the country.

We entrusted our life to this woman, and she failed us utterly.

37
Pandemic: Ealing, London

A navy blue coach boatneck dress, worn with silver disc earrings with the silhouette of Africa cut from them.

A new disease is spreading. I am a Politics student at heart, and read the news compulsively, so I follow it from the beginning – and am scared easily. I argue with David on Valentine's Day about the seriousness of what's happening, and whether it will reach us or our loved ones back home in South Africa.

I bring it up at work that we may need a plan, but it is dismissed. Everyone thinks I'm overreacting.

But it continues to spread. One Friday, I am helping to plan a response to how it could affect our businesses, and that afternoon suddenly, by no fault of my boss, my job is gone.

The life we'd just begun to touch is lost. The messaging from the government is so unclear about how to stay safe that, when lockdown is declared in South Africa, we follow those rules. I am once again, home-bound, and David is, thankfully, furloughed so we still have an income. He goes to the shops when absolutely necessary, and I make one trip to the pharmacy where we buy our first masks (and plastic gloves). South

Africa is on a newly created red list now. Somehow, I am even further from home than before. We postpone the big family wedding we'd been planning in South Africa, that I'd been holding onto to make up for the tiny civil ceremony we'd held here. Some days, it feels like my panic has spun out to become the world's – all the things my traumatised brain perceives as threats suddenly are just that: people, crowded places, enclosed spaces.

One afternoon, when my mother-in-law has finally convinced us to leave the flat to go as far as the overgrown back garden, I am doing morning pages, trying to process it all once again, and it comes to me – a sliver of an idea, slinking back in, nudging at the unthinkable boundary in my head. My degree can only be suspended for a year, and I am coming up on that deadline. I would not have quit my job to finish. But here I am, suddenly presented with nothing but time. Maybe I can finish my master's. I contact Julia, the supervisor who saved my life by suggesting I suspend my degree. She has put no pressure on me to resume but is glad to hear I am considering it. Usually, Oxford would require me to be physically present to complete. But Covid has changed that. Suddenly, I can finish from the relative safety of our flat in Ealing. But it involves returning to the work that is now embedded in traumatic memory for me. It involves more panic attacks, extra appointments for virtual Trauma Tapping therapy, and higher anti-anxiety medication doses. David is sent back to work much sooner than expected, so it is me alone in the flat, with my work and the cat. By the time I submit my final dissertation, I have nothing left. I pass but my research is not well-received by the markers at Oxford. They have not taken into account my exceptional circumstances form about my health, that Julia encouraged me to submit – and have marked me down for having someone assist me with my archival research.

The good news comes later. My lecturer from Rhodes University, Professor Siphokazi Magadla, who taught me about African feminism, knows about my dissertation topic and has faith in my academic rigour. She invites me to present my research on Dr Nkosazana Dlamini-Zuma's time in exile at a virtual colloquium. Hosted by the Centre for Women and Gender Studies at Nelson Mandela University in collaboration with Rhodes University and the University of Pretoria, the event is entitled *Inyathi ibuzwa kwabaphambili*, a Xhosa proverb meaning wisdom is learned or sought from the elders. I tell her I would be honoured, but also have to be honest with her about what the markers said. She smiles, and says simply, "Nica, they are not your audience."

I wear my navy-blue Coast dress that Sandhya gifted me when I started working at Make It Ealing, and silver disc earrings with the shape of Africa hollowed out in the centre– which I bought at a market in Windhoek, Namibia, with my then partner.

David sits off to the side, beaming with pride. I sit on my couch in Ealing, and because of the miracle of Zoom, I am able to share from these distant shores my painstaking research into the timeline of Dr Dlamini-Zuma's life in exile with a community of South African academics who are, quite simply, thrilled to hear it.

My graduation day falls in one of the periods of opening up. You could not pay me to go anywhere near Oxford, but we go for lunch and a picnic in Walpole Park. I wear my white cotton crossover dress with blue embroidery that I bought in Oxford, when David gifted me money to go shopping for my birthday. I have my degree. This isn't a story that says: it was worth it. It wasn't. If I were to go back in time, I cannot say I'd make the same choice. Only a masochist would.

But during the degree, when my field of vision had narrowed so many times, and I didn't remember what it was like to see the horizon, I firmly believed that degree was the last thing I was ever going to do. I'd accepted that. It's why I kept going when I really should have stopped. If this was going to be the last thing I ever did, I was going to bloody finish it.

Then, when I suspended the degree, I made peace with the fact that I'd never get it – that I'd chosen my life over it. So, unexpectedly having my degree – and my life – has meaning.

38
Elegance in Ealing continued: Ealing, London

A cream Patrizia Pepe sweater with bell sleeves and aubergine straight cut jeans from Monsoon.

We cannot do physical photoshoots during Covid, with the shop shut for lockdowns. Instead, an illustrator from the London College of Fashion, Chia-Hsuan Fan, gets in touch. Her graduate project focused on promoting London's fabulous charity and vintage clothing shops as an antidote to fast fashion, and she's a fan of our campaign. She creates a gorgeous series of artworks based on two of our photoshoots, one with a volunteer posing at the shop and another with a local actress posing amid the autumn leaves in Walpole Park.

39
A visa: Ealing, London

Plum winter boots, a puffy black jacket and a red and gold pashmina my mom bought me years ago.

Another strange blessing from this terrifying, and for so many people terrible, time comes. Because of Covid, the hearings are now online – and the waiting list is moving more quickly. Our appeal hearing is moved up to the autumn of this year. We've had time to sort out the things we'd gotten wrong the first time because of our lawyer. I've gritted my teeth through another English test.

Even though the judge cannot see anything below my chest, I put on high black stilettos (that I no longer wear out of the house due to my lack of faith in my legs) and fake pearl drop earrings for confidence. He rules in our favour in a matter of minutes, even noting how the strain of the process must have exacerbated my health condition. I swap my heels for plum winter boots, throw on a puffy black jacket and a red and gold pashmina my mom bought me years ago. We go to Walpole Park and simply walk in the autumn sunshine.

The goslings I've watched, since the very day they were born and a heron tried to snatch one away, have just begun to fly.

When I have words again, I write this poem *Two Geese*:

> *O friend, when you go to Gao make a detour by*
> *   Timbuktu & murmur my name to my friends*
> *& bring them a greeting perfumed with an exile*
> *that yearns after the soil where its friends, family &*
> *neighbours reside – Ahmed Baba al-Timbukti*
>
> *In my land of home*
> *I flinch from birds*
> *see only sharp beaks and talon hands*
> *baby brother's indian myna, named for a pirate, spits*
> *   "fuck you" and stalks me*
> *reaching for my trembling feet's soft souls*
> *everyone crows at his verbosity*
> *until he slits my mother's cheekbone.*
> *Her baby brother says, "it means he likes you"*
> *what they tell the little girl when a boy first hurts her*
> *But in a land of swanning falsehood*
> *adoration folds from me*
> *to the frantic ducklings and ungainly moorhens,*
> *the graciously lethal heron*
> *I am enchanted by canadian geese*
> *she nesting in shade*
> *he quietly on guard*
> *making still life*
> *I join him daily, a second sentry,*
> *until the spell cracks open*
> *three yellow fluffy prayers*
> *so foreign to their parents' chic*
> *I no longer flinch from birds*
> *I see bodies moulded for flight*

lifting into the wide sky
swallow your gavel Home Secretary
parents pairing for life
pillows of babies nestling together
mother goose ate from my hand once,
Unafraid &
Free.[1]

40
Conclusion: London, England

On 4 January 2023, I marry David at our big South African wedding, rooted in our community of 70 of our friends and family. It's just over three years since our civil ceremony in Haringey – where I'd worn blue, purposefully saving white for our other big day. My baby sister, an excellent baker, has been plotting the dessert all that time (with extensive practice, diagrams and voice notes). Finally, she prepares three flavours of croquembouche across three different sites. My mother-in-law, who loves to decorate cakes, crafts a Table Mountain cake with a giant version of me and David. She's convinced I wore a polka dot dress on the date we're commemorating, so mini-me is dressed in a red dress with white polka dots. I, however, remember the shorts I was wearing because there have been few phases of my life in which I had the confidence to wear shorts. My best friend's husband officiates. My father's fabulous band plays. As a surprise – he plays the jazz standard *Nica's Dream* for which I am named.

The night before, I sleep in a French white cotton nightgown with satin string ties up the side – a gift from my aunt. The day of, while getting ready, I wear a white satin dressing gown with lace inserts – a gift from my cousin. My bridesmaid, and high school friend, creates my bouquet from beautiful indigenous flora and fauna, augmenting the proteas and succulents with red roses. This red is picked up by my bright red strappy sandals, bought on a trip to the South African department store Woolworths with my big cousin. It also matches my red lipstick, done by the same big cousin. She pairs it with shimmery pale golden eyeshadow, black eyeliner and mascara. Another cousin curls my hair, pinning back a few strands into a demi chignon, before adding a pearl headpiece on top bought by my mother via Etsy from a South African jeweller. These pearls match the pearls dotted on my long veil, and the strand of pearls worn as a bracelet – gifted by my mother-in-law, who wore them on her wedding day. Lastly, they pick up on the mother of pearl and labradorite earrings that I bought when I was 16, swearing I'd wear them at my wedding, and before today wearing them at my civil ceremony. Sandhya and her husband, who served as my witnesses then, have flown from England to attend this wedding of ours as well.

I wear a white wedding gown from the Birmingham branch of David's Bridal. I choose it with the help of my cousin who is present in the room at the wedding dress shop and playing paparazzi for the WhatsApp group bridal party that are following from the other side of the world: my mom, my baby sister, my cousins and friends. The warmth and diversity of the people in Birmingham are such that it occurs to me I may have assimilated in England if I'd moved here instead of Oxford for university.

The day I buy my dress in Birmingham, I've already scoped the one I want – a ballgown with a Bardot neckline – for years. But I am determined to try multiple styles, which I actually enjoy doing, with the kindness of the lovely Brummie assistant. This is miraculous in itself – to enjoy dressing, which has become the period when I'm most likely to have a panic attack. Never mind doing it somewhat in public. On this day, it is probably a blessing that there is only one other, very supportive, voice in the room. I've got the support of my crowd in the form of messages to enjoy later, but I can only handle so many feelings and opinions at once.

I don't have to be told to walk slowly when she fans the ballgown skirt out behind me. Walking fast, feeling my heartbeat and breath change even infinitesimally, is still enough to bring on a panic attack – with the memories of regular attacks on the street in London and Oxford still living wedged in my nervous system and body. The humiliation and horror of being that vulnerable in an alien place has yet to leave me. But on this sunny day in Birmingham, I catch sight of the woman in a wedding gown in the mirrors as I spin around, and she is walking with grace.

Notes

Chapter 1
1. This poem has since been published in Mwanaka Media & Publishing's *Best New African Poets Anthology 2019* and my debut poetry collection *a sky is falling* in 2023.

Chapter 5
1. Since renamed Gqeberha.

Chapter 24
1. Previously published in *Taint Taint Taint Magazine* in 2021 and *a sky is falling*.

Chapter 39
1. Previously published in *Fixing Earth: Africa, UK & Ireland Writers Volume II* in 2022 and *a sky is falling*.

Suggested discussion topics

1. What was the role of Elegance in Ealing in the author's recovery?
2. Chart your life through your relationship with dress. This could be expressed in the written word or visually.
3. What role does place play in relation to the author's experience of distress?
4. How does the author experience dependence in relation to others?

References

Barr, S. (2019). 'Natalie Portman Says Women Have Been "Socialised to Believe That We're Not Feeling Angry", | *the Independent* [online]. Available at: https://www.independent.co.uk/life-style/women/natalie-portman-women-times-up-harpers-bazaar-interview-thor-a9025491.html

University of Fort Hare (2025). History, About Us [online]. Available at: https://www.ufh.ac.za/about-us#History

University of Oxford (2022). Academic Dress [online]. www.ox.ac.uk. Available at: https://www.ox.ac.uk/students/academic/dress

Index

disability. vi, xiv, 22, 71, 72, 91

dress. vi, xi, xii, xiv, 4, 9, 12, 14, 47, 53, 73, 79, 81, 82, 83, 85, 86, 90, 91, 95, 96, 97, 98, 99, 105, 107, 112, 122, 123, 124, 127, 131, 132, 135, 141, 142, 143, 144, 145, 146, 149, 151, 152, 159, 160, 164, 165

Elegance in Ealing. viii, ix, 79, 82, 95, 98, 99, 100, 105, 122, 139, 141, 143, 145, 146, 153, 164

foreign. 21, 39, 47, 64, 72, 86, 111, 112, 121, 135, 156

illness. vi, viii, 20, 23, 47, 53, 64, 71, 91, 93, 111

immigration. vi, xiv, 128, 138, 139, 148

marriage. viii, 85, 86, 121

medication. 13, 29, 44, 67, 68, 69, 102, 112, 150

panic. vi, 20, 27, 29, 33, 34, 35, 36, 39, 58, 59, 63, 68, 72, 89, 90, 102, 109, 111, 122, 137, 144, 150, 161

PTSD. vi, 63

second-hand. vi, 62

trauma. x, xiv, 16, 35

www.ingramcontent.com/pod-product-compliance
Lightning Source LLC
Chambersburg PA
CBHW070807230426
43665CB00017B/2517